with
the
Heart

So here you are, preparing to teach kids at church.

How did you end up in a children's classroom, anyway? Check all answers that apply.

To be quite honest, many folks end up teaching for all the wrong reasons. But God still uses them in wonderful ways. Why? Because in no time at all, they fall in love with their kids. And more than anything else, kids want to be loved. They crave adult attention. And they have the most endearing ways of loving you back.

Before you know it, you're hooked on teaching. It's the shy waves you get during church. Little ones wrapping

The **Honesty Test**

○ Guilt.

○ There was no one else to teach and my child is in this class.

○ I love teaching kids.

○ Adult class is boring so I'd rather be here.

○ Someone took the time to teach me as a child and I want to give back.

○ Our children's ministry leader begged me and I owe her a favor.

○ I'm a kid at heart and I thought this was one thing I could do for God's kingdom.

○ My kids are in the program and I figure I need to do my part.

○ I am the children's ministry leader and I couldn't get anyone else to teach.

○ I took a wrong turn when I was looking for the rest room.

themselves around your knees when they pass you in the hall. Excitement that registers on the Richter Scale when kids proudly show off a cool craft they made in your class. Knock-you-over hugs from kids who adore you and aren't too cool to show it. The first smile from a sullen child you've been trying to win over for weeks. Sparkles of delight when kids walk into your room and see what great things you have in store. The first stirrings of awe when, as a group, kids learn that God really does answer prayer. Faith taking hold. Belief dawning. Young lives changing. Who can live without all that? The people sitting down the hall in the adult classes on systematic theology ought to have their heads examined.

Congratulations—you made it to the right place!

You get to teach kids. You get to leave an indelible impression on young lives. You get to shape their faith while their minds are still innocent and untainted by skepticism. Pity those poor sleepyheads who are at home in their robes and slippers reading the funnies and having their third cup of coffee. You made it to the action arena of God's kingdom. Good for you!

Moses

"Here am I. Send my brother."

Jonah

"I'd rather be fish fodder than preach to those Ninevites! Now where's a boat going in the opposite direction?"

Gideon

"I can't really see why you'd try to make a warrior out of a guy hiding in a winepress, so I'm just going to stick this fleece out here one more time…"

You know, you'll find a fair number of famous and influential Bible characters who responded with a notable lack of enthusiasm when God called them to their particular task.

There's some pretty good company in the ranks of the reluctant righteous!

Jesus himself has some words of encouragement for you.

Pause Point

Read Matthew 18:1–14.

What qualities of children did Jesus want his disciples to emulate?

- *What positive childlike qualities would Jesus find in you?*
- *In what ways would Jesus want you to be more childlike?*

HEARTS, BRAINS & GROWING PAINS

Hearts, Brains, and Growing Pains
  Terrific Teaching that Changes You and Your Kids

Contributing Authors: Mary Grace Becker, Jodi Hoch, Carolyn Hock, Lois Keffer, Susan Martins Miller, Dean Stone, Dawn Renee Weary

Edited by Lois Keffer and Susan Martins Miller

© 2000 Cook Communications Ministries. All rights reserved.
ISBN 0781436842

Cover and interior design by iDesignEtc.

Printed in the U.S.A.

● *How is it that welcoming a child in Jesus' name is like welcoming Jesus himself?*

We sometimes feel like telling people to grow up. Jesus told his disciples to grow down! It's likely that the disciples were jockeying for rank and position within the little group of 12. Imagine their shamefaced silence when Jesus beckoned a child to be their example.

Jesus emphasized in strong terms the **importance of ministering to children.** Yet, interestingly enough, children's ministry is a low-limelight calling. The worship leaders, musicians, pastors and board members get all the prime-time up-front stuff. If you're with kids, you're likely to be

> *Whoever welcomes a little child like this in my name welcomes me.*
> Matthew 18:5

stuck off in a basement or far-flung wing of the church building, or even tucked in a closet with the choir robes! But when you hear the words of Jesus, you realize that teaching these "little ones" gets premiere billing in the kingdom of heaven.

What's so GREAT about Kids?

God has entrusted you with his most precious asset: kids.

☼ **They're trusting.** Faith comes naturally. They realize their inability to cope with life and willingly put themselves in others' care. Observe the peace on the countenance of a sleeping child.

☼ **They're quick to forgive.** Grudge-holding is not natural to childhood. They forget and move on.

☼ **They're full of energy and enthusiasm.** (Remember what that feels like?) When they discover a good thing, everyone is going to hear about it. Sophistication and self-consciousness don't restrain their joyful spirits.

☼ **They're loving and fresh from God.** Their feelings are real and without pretension. They're hungry to know more about the God who created them and loves them.

☼ **They're impressionable.** If you earn their trust, they'll put great stock in what you say and do. Their minds are like jello that has not yet set. You have a chance to put in all the good stuff right now!

☼ **They're our future.** Christianity is never more than 30 years from extinction. In just a few years, they'll be the carriers and communicators of our faith.

The father of a teenager expressed some nervousness because his son had agreed to house-sit for the CEO of the dad's company. This rather complex house-sitting assignment included a couple of dogs and several aquariums. No small task! The father joked that for the sake of his job, he hoped the son didn't goof up. (We're happy to report that all the pets thrived and everyone lived happily ever after!)

> **Eighty-five**
> - **percent of all**
> - **people who**
> - **do not accept**
> - **Jesus Christ**
> - **by the age of**
> - **18 never**
> - **will.**

House-sitting involves accepting responsibility for the sum of another person's possessions. Think of teaching as soul-sitting. Step back for a moment and realize that God has entrusted you with the very future of his kingdom. **Each child who comes under your influence is an irreplaceable treasure to God.** A fragile bundle of potential. To use Jesus' own metaphor, a lamb for whom the shepherd would search far into the night.

An awesome privilege. Exciting! And scary. So you want to make the right preparations. You need to start with your H-E-A-R-T.

Humble yourself.

Feeling a little like a **jar of clay?** Good! That's just what God wants. Remember Jesus' words to the disciples? "Unless you humble yourself as a child…" The first thing every good children's worker learns is that teaching is a partnership with the Holy Spirit. You're playing doubles here, and no matter how gifted a teacher you are, you're by far the weaker partner. Start with a little fear and trembling and you're off on the right foot.

Examine yourself.

Take a serious look in the mirror. Look at yourself as if you were a

For God, who said, "Let light shine out of darkness," made his light shine in our hearts to give us the light of the knowledge of the glory of God in the face of Christ. But we have this treasure in jars of clay to show that this all-surpassing power is from God and not from us.

2 Corinthians 4:6–7

child coming to your class, seeing the teacher for the first time. **Try on your smile.** Is it warm? Does it go all the way to your eyes? Or does it look a bit half-hearted, strained or preoccupied? Your face tells a child so much about you. Experts estimate that eighty percent of our communication is nonverbal. As you search your face, ask the Lord to prepare your heart

As water reflects a face, so a man's heart reflects the man.
Proverbs 27:19

for his service. Let him sweep away cobwebs of unhealthy attitudes or grudges. Look at the person who was created in God's image. Ask him to cleanse you, to restore you and to fill you with true, contagious joy. Maybe you'll need to do this step more than once. Pray with the Psalmist, "Restore to me the joy of your salvation and grant me a willing spirit, to sustain me" (Psalm 51:12).

♡ ♡ ♡ ♡ ♡ ♡ ♡ ♡ ♡ ♡ ♡ ♡

Ask God to make you a pure conduit of his love.

Jesus stood and said in a loud voice, "If anyone is thirsty, let him come to me and drink. Whoever believes in me, as the Scripture has said, streams of living water will flow from within him."

John 7:37–38

Imagine a group of kids playing on a hot day. A neighbor gets out the hose to wash his car. "Squirt us! Squirt us!" the kids shout, skittering around the yard just in case he does. The neighbor gives a quick swish with the hose and all the kids scream and dance with glee. Oh, but you have so much more to offer than a refreshing squirt from a hose! The message of the Gospel is yours to share. **You are the conduit of the living water** Jesus spoke of. You need to disallow anything in your life that would restrict the flow of God's love through you to the kids he's put in your care. Ask the Lord to make every part of you pure and winsome—a vessel set apart for his use. You don't have to be outgoing or the life of the party or anything at all that you're not. Ask him give you his loving spirit that spills over to refresh and cheer everyone you touch. Kids are thirsty for that kind of love. And God has it for you to share in abundance.

♡ ♡ ♡ ♡ ♡ ♡ ♡ ♡ ♡ ♡ ♡ ♡

Reflect on your strengths and weaknesses.

In Christ we who are many form one body, and each member belongs to all the others. We have different gifts, according to the grace given us.... If it is serving, let him serve; if it is teaching, let him teach.

Romans 12:5, 6a, 7

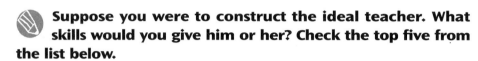 **Suppose you were to construct the ideal teacher. What skills would you give him or her? Check the top five from the list below.**

- ❏ Greeter
- ❏ Bible teacher
- ❏ storyteller
- ❏ craft leader
- ❏ artist
- ❏ prayer warrior
- ❏ singer
- ❏ listener
- ❏ discussion guide
- ❏ friend

Maybe you're all these things—good for you! Most of us aren't. So let's get this job description in perspective. Take a minute to think back to your childhood. List three teachers who made an impact on your life.

1.

2.

3.

Now look back at the "ideal teacher list." Did the teachers you listed possess all those skills? Probably not. God has us serve within a community of believers for a reason. In your church you may know a great guitar player who can get kids to sing their lungs out, but would never touch a bottle of glitter glue. Or **a craft princess who would freeze at the thought of telling a Bible story to a group of kids.** Get them on your team. Never hesitate to ask for help. Do a little groundwork—you'll be surprised at how many folks are delighted to lend a hand. "Hey, I'm teaching a kids' class this year and I've seen the great crafts you do…what a wonderful song leader you are…how terrific you are at acting. I wonder if you'd be willing to visit my class from time to time and help out."

Maybe you're a wonder teacher who's brimming with talent in all directions. Great! You'll love how teaching allows you to exercise every gift. But if you could use a little support in some areas, go for it. Let the Body of Christ engage in the care of its kids.

*T*rust God to do what he says he will.

Therefore, my dear brothers, stand firm. Let nothing move you. Always give yourselves fully to the work of the Lord, because you know that your labor in the Lord is not in vain.

1 Corinthians 15:58

Instant gratification is a hot concept in our culture. But it's not part of the expected benefits package when you teach kids. Plastic money has the potential to grant our whims. The TV remote, the microwave and ATMs get us what we want when we want it. (Do you remember when you had to plan an hour ahead to have a baked potato?)

Building godly character in kids is a long-term (read: eternal) investment. You may see quick results. Then again, you may not. In fact, some weeks when your class's energy level goes into hyperdrive, it may feel as if you've lost ground. To quote the famous Mr. Churchill: *Nevah, nevah, nevah, nevah give up!* Why? Because you have God's promise that your work is not in vain.

Jesus liked to use agricultural illustrations—let's go for one here.

*O*ne day a teacher put on her grubby clothes and went to dig a garden. She read all the garden books carefully and choose the right things for her zone. In her vegetable garden she planted a row of beans. Gentle rains came. Then the sunshine warmed the soft brown earth. In just a few days, the beans sprouted and the teacher rejoiced with great joy.

The teacher planted bulbs by a sheltering fence. She took great care to plant them at just the right depth, and she made sure the pointy part was up. She bought special fertilizer and sprinkled it lovingly around her bulbs before she covered them with rich soil. When the beans sprouted in her vegetable garden, the teacher ran to the fence to check her bulbs. No sprouts. When the beans grew heavy pods, she ran to the fence to check her bulbs. No sprouts. When the teacher cooked her beans with bacon and a touch of oregano there were still no sprouts on the bulbs. *Humph!* she thought. *See if I ever plant bulbs again. They cost me a lot and I got nothing.*

Months passed and a cold, bleak winter turned to hopeful signs of spring. The teacher wandered in her yard and considered her spring planting. Much to her surprise, rows of beautiful green sprouts greeted her by her sheltering fence. Within days they burst into a riot of color—yellow jonquils, silky red tulips and fragrant hyacinths. The teacher clapped her hands in delight. Then a late snowstorm blanketed the blooming flowers. When the sun came out and melted the snow, the teacher was afraid to look at the damage that had been done. Lo and behold, **the tulips, jonquils and hyacinths stood as strong and beautiful as ever.** Year after year the lovely tulips, jonquils and hyacinths bloomed and multiplied and brought joy to the teacher's heart.

So it is with teaching children. You're not planting seeds of godly character—you're planting bulbs! They may seem to lie dormant for a long time. But the Holy Spirit is doing his part. Someday you'll see fruit of your labor, and it will endure. It will multiply and many people will be touched by its beauty and grace. And then you will know that your teaching has not been in vain, for God has done just what he said he would.

Let us not become weary in doing good, for at the proper time we will reap a harvest if we do not give up. Therefore, as we have opportunity, let us do good to all people, especially to those who belong to the family of believers.

Galatians 6:9-10

To review, here's how to START WITH YOUR HEART.

Humble yourself.

Examine yourself.

Ask God to make you a pure conduit of his love.

Reflect on your strengths and weaknesses.

Trust God to do what he says he will.

Do you know what's really exciting about all this? In the midst of this process, you're taking good care of *you*. Your commitment to share God's love with your kids is going to give your own faith walk an incredible boost. Amidst all the hullaballo that's part of teaching kids, you may not even see how you're growing. But one day you'll wake up to the glorious knowledge that **Jesus is your friend** in a deeper way than he's ever been before.

You are my friends, if you do what I command. I no longer call you servants, because a servant does not know his master's business. Instead, I have called you friends, for everything that I learned from my Father I have made known to you. You did not choose me, but I chose you and appointed you to go and bear fruit—fruit that will last.

John 15:14–16a

2

Go for the Godpront

Eleven-year-old Adam's mind was everywhere but on the lesson.

But in a Bible story drama, he'd performed reasonably well as Joseph, proudly wearing the ragged oriental robe as the famed coat of many colors.

"Why were Joseph's brothers jealous of him?" the teacher asked, hopeful that Adam's involvement in the story would spur a thoughtful answer.

"Because when Joseph was little he was kidnapped by the Russians and taken to a space station," Adam answered with a perfectly straight face.

The teacher swallowed and took another shot. "I bet you can come up with a better answer than that."

Adam rolled his eyes. "Yep," he said finally. "It was space aliens, not Russians."

Of course, the rest of the class was vastly entertained. The teacher pushed on doggedly. "Did somebody else ever get something *you* really wanted?"

The light went on in Adam's face. "Yeah! My neighbor got a trampoline and I always wanted one." Ah…first base.

"Do you suppose Joseph had something his brothers wanted?"

"Um…yeah. He got all the attention from his dad. And he didn't have to go to the far fields to take care of the sheep. And besides that he had all these dreams where he was more important."

Bingo! Somewhere behind all the buzz and distortion, Adam really was tuned in. He had a different way of coming at things than most kids—a unique learning style that had caused him to fail repeatedly at school. But his Sunday school teacher was determined that Adam wouldn't feel like a failure in God's house. Every week he required about three extra doses of encouragement.

"I don't like putting things together."

"But I'll bet you're good at it. Just give it a try. I'll make the first two cuts for you." Result: an admirable Bible story craft.

"I can't draw."

"Don't worry about making a pretty picture. Just show what your answer to prayer was." Result: Adam's stick figures portrayed stress over taking a test, then receiving a passing grade.

"I'm not good at saying Bible verses."

"Okay—how about singing it? Let's work out a tune and some motions." Result: Adam performed with all the grace of a stick mop, but he was humming the song two weeks later.

One Sunday Adam's mom caught the teacher in a hallway. "Adam just *loves* your class," she reported. "I know he's…well, he's different. But he's never been so excited about church. He always tells us what happened in class. We're just so happy!"

The grateful teacher walked away in a bit of a daze, then pumped her fist in the air. The extra effort was paying off. Sunday school was a place where Adam could spread his wings without having them clipped. He liked coming to God's house. *Yes!*

What made the difference? Instead of sticking with traditional "pour and store" teaching, Adam's teacher made a commitment to **go for the Godprint.**

Go for the what? Let's do what any great teacher would do: ask questions to get to the answer.

On average, how much teaching time do you have with your kids each week? Don't count settling in time, clean-up, or trips to the drinking fountain. Estimate your solid, face-to-face teaching time.

During that time, what do you want to accomplish? Prioritize this list. *(Warning: this is a tough one.)*

My Priority List

___ Teach what the Bible says.

___ Establish a nurturing relationship with your kids.

___ Pray for each child and teach them to pray for and with each other.

___ Help kids understand how to live out Bible truths.

___ Teach kids how to use their Bibles.

___ Help kids memorize key Bible verses.

___ Have meaningful personal interaction with each child.

___ Help kids discover the delight of being in God's house.

___ Motivate kids to take charge of their journey of faith.

___ Help children know God; provide opportunities when they can come face-to-face with God's power and plans for their lives.

___ Give opportunities for kids to accept Jesus as their Savior and grow in the Christian walk.

___ Get through the curriculum lesson.

___ Make sure the Bible truths you teach make it out of the classroom.

___ All of the above.

This chapter will serve as a guide to help you untangle this daunting list of expectations so **you can leave class every week with confidence that you've used your precious time wisely** and done the very best job with your class.

Your Faith Journey

 What started you on the road toward a personal relationship with God?

- ❏ a stirring sermon
- ❏ an evangelistic crusade
- ❏ reading the Bible
- ❏ 47 verses of "Just As I Am"
- ❏ a stimulating theological discussion
- ❏ loving and being loved by someone who knew God

Most of us are drawn to the Lord by someone whose love for God is contagious—someone who knows how to express that special love in winsome ways. Infectious Christians have a way of leaving Godprints on the lives of those around them. When we teach, we need to ask God for that uncommon grace—that ability to touch children's lives so they're ready to open their hearts to God's transforming power.

Pause Point

Three unforgettable people who've left Godprints in my life.

1.

2.

3.

When you're with your kids, **the most important thing you can do is leave a Godprint on their lives.** You can—and need to—teach Bible facts and work on memory verses. But facts and words alone don't change lives. God changes lives. God speaks through people like you to bring his Word to life and to make himself known. You're the Gospel in shoes.

> 66 *The relationship you build with your*
> ● *students is the foundation for every other*
> ● *good thing that happens in your class.* 99

In Christian education we're not simply in the business of transferring information. We're in our classrooms to guide children toward God. What we're really pursuing is our students' spiritual formation. As Dr. Catherine Stonehouse says in her excellent book, *Joining Children on the Spiritual Journey:*

"The goal of spiritual formation is a maturing faith and a deepening relationship with Jesus Christ, through which we become more like Christ in the living of our everyday lives in the world. The spiritual life is formed through practices that help to open the person to God and break down barriers that hinder his or her perception of God. Spirituality involves the whole person relating to God and is not something laminated onto life. True spirituality has an impact on every part of a person's being and is expressed through the personality in all relationships" (p. 21).

A Child's Faith Journey

Each child develops according to a unique, God-given pattern. We need to do everything we can to understand and respect that pattern!

God created KIDS to develop:

Physically • Emotionally • Socially
Intellectually • Spiritually

Human development and spiritual formation are not two separate, unconnected processes. In children's ministry we need to think of the whole child. Our teaching needs to touch each area of their lives. Think of it this way: you can't water one stalk of a growing plant. **You water the whole plant.** It grows deep roots, a strong stem, glossy leaves, and eventually the plant blooms. So it is with children. We minister to the whole child in order for the child to thrive.

> "For I know the plans I have for you," declares the Lord, "plans to prosper you and not to harm you, plans to give you hope and a future."
>
> Jeremiah 29:11

Researchers have learned that a child's personality and receptivity to God are formed very early in life. Healthy personality development plays a huge role in preparing children for ongoing openness to God. So when you choose children's ministry materials, keep the whole child in mind. Your teaching resources need to:

- *allow children to move and meet physical challenges,*

- *teach children to recognize their God-given emotions and express them in appropriate ways,*

☀ *help children develop social skills through interaction with their peers,*

☀ *stimulate children's minds with new thoughts about what it means to live out God's Word, and*

☀ *introduce children to who God is and how he can transform their lives.*

Observing the way children develop allows us to predict what they'll be ready to learn at certain ages and states. (Check out Chapter 4 for an overview of child development and what to expect from the kids in your class.) However, as much as we've grown to know about children and how they learn, it's good to remind ourselves that God doesn't work on any human schedule! **We need to take time to discover what's wonderfully unique about each child in our care.** Like Adam's teacher, we need to probe until our questions strike a chord in their spirits and understanding dawns in their souls.

It all boils down to this amazing fact (amazing in that it comes from a curriculum publisher): your goal in those precious few minutes that you have with your kids is not to get all the way through the lesson. **Your goal is to create a moment in time when God can touch a child's life.** A well-constructed lesson will give you meaty Bible content presented in a relational format that meets the needs of all kinds of kids. A lot to ask? Not when you consider what hangs in the balance.

♡ ♡ ♡ ♡ ♡ ♡ ♡ ♡ ♡ ♡ ♡

Teachable Moments

It's possible for a child to absorb a great deal of information about the Bible without learning to know who God is and choosing to walk in his steps. Kids need to know not just what God says in his Word—they need to know God himself. When you present Bible stories, focus on Godprints: how God's presence and power impacts Bible characters' lives.

We encounter Godprints as we discover who God is. We see his character revealed in Scripture, in creation, in relationships within a Christian community and ultimately within ourselves. Godprints are:

• **Evidence of God at work in circumstances, in individuals, and in the community.** *"I see that God was here."*

• **The imprint of his character that God leaves on our lives as we learn to know him.** *"As I learn about God, I believe in him and love him. Because I love him, I want to be like him. I see how God is active in my life and changing me to be like him."*

The Godprints Test

As you approach each lesson, ask,

● How can I tell this Bible story so that my kids will learn who God is?

● In this story, what's the evidence that God was here?

● How did God make a difference to the people in this story?

● How does God want to make a difference in our lives today?

What do we want for our kids? For them to know God, love God, put their faith in Jesus and grow in godly character. We want Godprints to spill over into every area of their lives! Openness to God isn't something we can program. But we can focus on building relationships with our kids so we're sensitive to those teachable moments when they occur. God's love is irresistible. It's powerful. It's transforming. When you teach, go for the Godprint!

> *And we, who with unveiled faces all reflect the Lord's glory, are being transformed into his likeness with ever-increasing glory, which comes from the Lord, who is the Spirit.*

2 Corinthians 3:18

The Power of God's Story

God has spoken in his Word through story. It is through story that we come to understand the awesome character of God, love him and long to be in relationship with him. The marvelous thing about the Bible is that we can draw from its well of stories again and again. For they are more than just stories—they're God's truth.

At each stage of development, kids (and adults!) learn something new from the "old, old story." But we need to tell those stories in new, new ways! Invest in becoming a great storyteller. Practice your Bible story presentation in front of a mirror. Play to your kids' love of the dramatic and fascination with mystery.

8 tips for great Storytelling

Immerse yourself in the story until it's part of you. Don't start with what's in your teacher guide—start with the Bible. Read the story in several translations. Start early in the week so it has time to sink in.

Be excited. If you're bored with a story, your kids are bound to be bored too. Your excitement is just as contagious. Consciously crank your energy level up five or ten notches when you're set to tell the Bible story. Pour yourself into it.

Be in close proximity to your listeners. Remove barriers. Move around. Don't be afraid to get right in a child's face. Your interaction with kids will keep them on the edge of their seats.

Make eye contact with everyone. Let your eyes rest on one individual for a few seconds, then move onto another. Don't fall into the trap of focusing in one direction. Let your eyes grow large, squinty, skeptical, or roll them. Your eyes are second only to your voice in communicating.

Experiment with your voice. Pinch your nose for a nasal sound. Speak with an accent for certain characters. Even if your accent is pretty lame, kids will love it. Use your entire vocal range. Try a high, squeaky "What???" and a low, growly "That was the wro-o-o-ng choice." Record yourself, then listen. How much variety of tone do you produce?

Make your face rubber. Practice in the mirror making all the extreme faces you can think of. Practice fury, delight, surprise and wonder. Even if you're not normally a terribly expressive person, you'll be surprised at the fun faces you can produce.

Make a variety of approaches. Become a character. Be a mouse in the corner. Be a narrator. Be a cheerleader. Do anything but the same thing each week. Make it easy on yourself and choose children's ministry material with a rich variety of storytelling techniques.

Use simple props. You'd be amazed at what you can do with a large scarf, a walking stick or a noisemaker. Props transform you into someone else and fascinate kids.

The Bible is a wondrous book. Children need the opportunity to enter, not simply hear, God's stories. When you process stories, don't go for simple, prepackaged answers. And avoid "guess what's in my mind" questions. Use follow-up questions that kids can't answer with one word. Make them dig for answers that will give meaning and direction in their lives. Approach Scripture with a sense of wonder and mystery and allow kids to discover its life-building truths for themselves.

Don't rush through God's Word! Each story is so rich in meaning. Give kids more than one hurried week to find the truth in a Bible story and practice living out that truth. Present a story yourself one week. The next week, let kids teach it back. Take advantage of their natural tendency to "ham it up." As a teacher, you know that you're the one who learns the most. Let kids enjoy the benefits of teaching as well. Taking responsibility for a story presentation will solidify a story in a child's mind as nothing else can.

When kids teach a story, encourage them to use their imaginations. We Christians have backed away from imagination for too long. We feel safer sticking to the dry facts. Guess what? **Imagination is God's gift to children.** Children can't understand all the complexities of Scripture. It's not even appropriate to encourage them to try. God gave kids imaginations to "fill in the blanks" in their understanding. Imagination plays a key role as children stretch to understand the stories of the Bible and God's involvement in their lives.

♡ ♡ ♡ ♡ ♡ ♡ ♡ ♡ ♡ ♡ ♡

A Community That Disciples

The Father in heaven is not willing that any of these little ones should be lost," says Jesus. That's interesting. In some churches, adults are less than receptive to the noise and spontaneity that children bring to the scene. They wish rowdy children would "get lost"! Do you see a conflict with Jesus' priorities?

Don't let your church get its priorities discombobulated! Moral development in children is more than instruction about what is right and wrong. Children learn from seeing others in a Christian community resolving moral conflicts as they work and struggle to apply biblical truth to their lives.

Effective moral education begins with teachers and parents listening to children, not merely talking to them. **Children need to see moral**

reasoning in action in the lives of the adults around them. They are able to see and comprehend mature moral decision-making before they can understand it from a verbal perspective or verbalize it themselves.

God's plan for children's spiritual development encompasses a community of faith. We see this commanded and demonstrated in the books of the Law though the rituals and festivals of the people of Israel. The very life of the Jewish family and community centered around sharing and **celebrating** with rich sensory experiences the great stories of faith and God's ongoing presence in their midst. Now as then, the classroom is not the primary place where faith is learned. It is grasped in the larger, more diverse context of a faith community.

Who participates in this community? Parents, first of all. Teachers, certainly. But don't forget the host of others from the greeters at the door to the grandmas who run the church kitchen. Each person within a group of believers needs to consciously surround the children of the community with a loving willingness to disciple. Kids, in turn, need those faithful adults and teenagers who consciously cultivate relationships with them. Within the community of faith, **kids need to find models whom they love, admire, want to attach to, and imitate.** Participation in community is essential to healthy spiritual growth at every stage of life.

A Christian community embraces the authoritative story of the Bible as the master story of our faith. Then members of the community weave their own story and personal experiences into God's master story. Living in a faith community means sharing the story of the Bible as well as our individual stories. Children watch and learn. In the best faith communities, children watch, *participate,* and learn.

Within the faith community, children need opportunities to serve. Too often kids remain solely on the receiving end. In fact, they need to give back. Service plays a key role in spiritual formation. A desire to serve others grows as Christ-like character develops. Choose children's ministry materials that offer options for service. Watch **kids take pride in doing their part** and making a contribution to the community. Letting kids discover that they can make a difference is one of the most invaluable gifts we can give them.

Worship

Young children can meet God in authentic ways, although they may not be the same as an adult's encounter with God. It's a mistake to think that we have to bombard kids with programming that moves at the same frenetic pace as the media. Yes, they're a media generation. And that's exactly why they need space and time for quiet reflection and worship.

A well-paced children's program provides a balance of lively activity and quiet moments when children can experience God in worship. Simple rituals and sensory-rich, tactile experiences help children focus on worship. Use soft music, simple praise songs, a prayer corner with a Bible and a special rug, **candlelight,** prayers with a simple, repeated response and art experiences that express praise. Build a pause point into each lesson, even if it lasts only a few moments.

When you lead children in worship times, choose everyday words that children can understand. It's a challenge to avoid religious vocabulary loaded with symbolism and theological overtones. But it's a good challenge. And you'll get better at it as you practice.

Teacher, Mentor, Learner

Do you know someone who makes everyone smile just by walking into the room? **Who brings a positive, loving attitude to every situation?** Who is affirming without being syrupy and is always ready to give people the benefit of the doubt? Who absolutely brings out the best in everyone? *Be that person!*

Everyone has an impact on those around them. What's yours? Live your life in the fragrance of God's love. Give away tons of smiles—they're free! Even if you're feeling flatter than a fly swatter, God can give you energy and personal warmth. You may go home from teaching, **splat on your sofa and not move a muscle** for two hours, but give, give, give when you're with your kids. Very soon they'll be growing and giving back.

> 66 *Let kids know that God is your daily companion and that your relationship with him is vital and growing. Let them see how your faith impacts every area of your life.* 99

Share your own faith stories with your kids. If you're wrestling with a problem, let them pray for you. Tell about struggles you endured when you were their age and how God brought you through. Let kids know that God is your daily companion and that your relationship with him is vital and growing. Let them see how your faith impacts every area of your life.

And don't worry about being perfect. When you

blow it, say so. You won't lose an ounce of respect by saying, "I'm sorry I spoke harshly. I'm feeling crabby this morning. Will you forgive me?" Kids will love and respect you all the more.

Realize that sometimes you'll be the learner. God's Spirit is at work in the lives of your kids. Their insights and grace may surprise you. What fun! We're all on a faith journey. It doesn't end until heaven. So, pilgrim, come alongside those kids in your care. Share your journey and grow together.

Give your kids the gift of a rich, accepting environment where they can learn and grow at the pace that is best for them. To go for the Godprint, give yourself to your kids. Use a balance of formats and instructional strategies that honor their faith development. Each child in your class needs to feel welcomed, cherished and understood. Make it your goal for all your students to say, "I rejoiced with those who said to me, 'Let us go to the house of the LORD'" (Psalm 122:1).

Chapter

3

Say Good-bye to Saturday Night Fever

(and Sunday mornings at the supermarket)

*T*his chapter is going to make your life better. Really. Let's start with a quick personal inventory. Check all that apply.

Did you make more than a couple of check-marks in this list? Did you check everything? It's time for a change! Take a deep breath and read on.

The fact is, our lives are so busy that the majority of us find ourselves scrambling on Saturday night to get ready for Sunday's lesson. Saturday Night Fever runs rampant among children's ministry volunteers. We all have good intentions. This week was going to be different. You had every

My Personal Inventory

○ My schedule feels out of control.

○ I'm always running behind and scrambling to cover details.

○ I resent not being able to spend time on the things that matter most.

○ On more than one occasion I've done my teaching preparation in the car on the way to church.

○ I speed-read my teacher guide, then come away without a clue.

○ I've turned my pantry upside down looking for last-minute craft ideas.

○ I race by the supermarket on the way to church to pick up supplies I didn't realize I needed.

intention of breaking out the teacher guide early in the week. Then life happened. Aaargh! Now the alarms go off, and you shift into hyperdrive to get everything done.

How Do I Feel When. . .

I wait until the last minute
to prepare to teach?

I'm well prepared
ahead of time?

There is a more excellent way, a way that gives peace of mind. A way that gives kids a teacher who's focused on them, rather than on, "Now, what was I supposed to do next?"

Creating spaces in your week for thoughtful and productive lesson preparation is not as difficult as you might think.

♡ ♡ ♡ ♡ ♡ ♡ ♡ ♡

> 66 **If the devil**
> ● **can't make you**
> ● **bad, he'll make**
> ● **you busy.** 99
> ●
> ● *Corrie Ten Boom*

Preventive Medicine

There's a simple, effective vaccine for Saturday Night Fever. The main ingredient? The mind of Christ.

You would be hard pressed to find a person who teaches children out of selfish ambition or conceit! But once you've made the commitment to teach children, your challenge is to give the right priority to the things of God. **There is an enemy who would like to keep you dazed, confused and a step behind yourself.** Don't cooperate with him! Instead, approach your teaching with the mind of Christ: humility, obedience, self-sacrifice and a focus on glorifying God in your service.

Determine to focus your mind on Christ.

What does he desire for each child? When you ask God to give you the mind of Christ, expect to give your best. God will be faithful.

The Mind of Christ

Do nothing out of selfish ambition or vain conceit, but in humility consider others better than yourselves. Each of you should look not only to your own interests, but also to the interests of others. Your attitude should be the same as that of Christ Jesus.

Philippians 2:3–5

You will have peace. Your children will thrive. God will be honored.

♡ ♡ ♡ ♡ ♡ ♡ ♡ ♡ ♡ ♡ ♡

Early Preparation Is a Win-Win

The Mind of Christ

Seek first his kingdom and his righteousness, and all these things will be given to you as well.

Matthew 6:33

The hardest part of lesson preparation is just getting started. There are lots of good reasons and good ways to get over that bump. Having the mind of Christ motivates us to do the best teaching we can. That includes being more than barely a step ahead of the kids. Check out the benefits of jump-starting your lesson prep early in the week.

☑ You'll sleep better.

☑ Kids will learn more.

☑ Parents will appreciate you.

☑ You'll have a gentle, quiet spirit.

☑ You'll be nicer to your family on Saturday.

☑ You can spend Saturday night with family or friends.

☑ You'll teach better.

☑ Kids will behave better.

☑ You'll have time to delegate.

☑ God will be glorified.

Maybe the idea of being on top of the game enough to **delegate parts of the lesson** has never occurred to you. Think about it! Teenagers can do a great job with crafts and games. Parents might welcome the opportunity to stop by and help with treats, just so they can see what's going on in their kids' class. Invite a retired member of your congregation to dress up as a Bible character and help act out the story. (How many times have you found this suggestion in your lesson material on Saturday night when it's too late to call someone?)

Inviting a helper to teach part of the lesson not only eases your load—it helps others build relationships with your kids. It provides a supportive environment for first-timers in children's ministry to get their feet wet. They may have so much fun they will want to help you every week!

♡ ♡ ♡ ♡ ♡ ♡ ♡ ♡ ♡ ♡ ♡

Create Your Plan

Being stuck in a rut of Saturday night preparation doesn't mean you have to stay there. **You can climb out.** And there's no model method that's right for everyone. While early preparation is the goal, several routes will get you there—and all of them will give you back your Saturday nights. Choose the plan that works best with your personality and household schedule.

Master your moments.

Put your teacher guide and a pen or highlighter in a spot where you can grab a few moments here and there. Buy yourself an inexpensive copy holder to set it at an angle that's easy for hands-off reading.

- Next to your computer. Read a portion of your lesson as you wait for your e-mail to boot up or wait for the printer to churn out 18 pages.

- In the car. Plan while you wait to pick up kids from school or soccer practice.

- By the phone. Use precious minutes while you are "on hold" to get prepared.

- By the bathroom sink. Read a snippet of your lesson while you floss.

- Next to the kitchen sink. Prop it up and choose activities or memorize a verse while the coffee brews, the toast toasts and the microwave zaps.

Good spots for my teacher guide:

✪

✪

✪

Deliver a Monday lunch punch.

Give Saturday night stress a knock-out punch by using your lunch hour on Monday to get going on the next week's lesson. Make it a treat for yourself—something you'll look forward to each week. Pick up a sandwich or pack a lunch and go to a park. Or take yourself to lunch at a restaurant or coffee shop with an inviting atmosphere (and a nice selection of desserts). Ask to be seated in a quiet corner where you can read and reflect on your lesson without interruption. Who knows? When you become a regular, you may have opportunities to share your faith with the restaurant staff. If you have a team teacher, perhaps you may want to set a weekly lunch date and prepare together as you deepen your friendship.

If this method sounds good to you, get a special folder or tote bag for your teacher guide. Get a really fun pen and a fresh highlighter that you use only for lesson preparation.

Make a divine appointment.

Set aside an evening early in the week and

- put on comfy clothes
- light a candle
- put on instrumental praise music
- get a cup of tea or hot chocolate
- bring your Bible and favorite devotional book
- close a door (at least mentally!) on the rest of the world

My Pleasant Place

Where will I enjoy going each week to have lunch and read through my teacher guide?

My Team

Who do I need with me to plan?

Who can I ask to pray for me?

Let your family know that this is your special time with God. Have someone else answer the phone. See your lesson preparation time as a divine appointment, an opportunity for spiritual growth for yourself. As you learn more about God's plan for each child's life, you'll discover exciting things he's planned for you. You may want to keep a journal of the spiritual food you receive for yourself as you plan to teach children.

Ten minutes a day

If you're experiencing a time of "overwhelm" in your life, this approach may be best for you. Look for a pocket of time each day when you can **grab 10 minutes for lesson prep.** Do the daily steps listed below, and by Friday you'll have things well in hand!

• When can I keep this divine appointment?

• Where will I meet with God?

• What do I need with me when I meet God?

Monday: Read through the lesson, choose the best activities for your class and note the supplies you'll need. Add them to your grocery list.

Tuesday: Read the Bible story from the Bible, then from the teacher guide once more. Look at it from the perspective of how children can see what God desires for them.

Wednesday: Pray for your class. What are the kids struggling with right now? Jot down the Bible truth and memory verse from the lesson on a sticky note and put it on the fridge or a bathroom mirror.

Thursday: Memorize the verse and think about the Bible truth. What trait does God want to give your children through this Bible story? Double-check your supplies.

Friday: **Collect everything you'll need for Sunday morning and put it in a tote bag.** Set the bag in a convenient place where you won't forget it. Do a quick scan of the lesson to set it in your mind.

Saturday: Celebrate the fact that you're prepared! Pray for each child in your class.

Sunday: Focus on your kids and enjoy them! Ask God to shine through you.

Just how effective is it to do something for only 10 minutes a day? Researchers asked people who had never juggled before to test two approaches. After an equal amount of instruction, one group practiced once a week for an hour. The other group practiced 10 minutes a day, six days a week. After three weeks, guess which group was far ahead of the other? The 10-minutes-a-day group.

A college professor overheard a group of students moaning that they had an overwhelming study load. They couldn't possibly get the work done in the time they had. They were sitting around in the dining hall after lunch, passing the 25 minutes or so before their next class was scheduled to begin. The professor calmly explained that he was working on a new scholarly commentary on the Book of Matthew. Whenever he had just 15 minutes of unscheduled time, he worked on his book. The manuscript grew daily, in small pieces.

A young woman shared a ride to work in the mornings with her mother. If she was ready to leave five minutes early, the young woman grew restless. *Why not just go to work early?* she wondered. Her mother declined to leave early. Instead, she used those five minutes to sweep the kitchen or clear the clutter on the dining room table or take the newspapers out to the recycling tub or start a load of laundry. **Even five minutes was enough time to do something meaningful.**

Where are the pockets of empty time in your day?

- I think the 10-minutes-a-day plan could work for me. ◯ Yes ◯ No

- When can I find 10 minutes in my days?

Make it a Sabbath habit

We saved the best for last. This is the simplest, time-tested, tried-and-true way to leave Saturday Night Fever behind forever. Read through next week's lesson on Sunday afternoon. During the week that follows, you'll be amazed at how the Holy Spirit will bring to mind stories, ideas, songs, and experiences that relate to what you're planning to teach. You will be delighted how all the pieces will fit together. You'll find that your teaching flows out of what God is doing in your life.

Reading through my next lesson on Sunday afternoon is:

❏ Very doable. I'm going to start this plan.

❏ Most likely doable. Worth a try.

❏ Doable if I shuffle some things around.

21 Days to a New Habit

However you choose to do it, plan your work and work your plan. God deserves your best effort. So do his children. Whether you work best in long blocks of time, or 10 minutes a day, make lesson preparation a priority. The rewards are as precious as a child's hug, a pat on the back, a heavenly crown.

Researchers have determined that it takes **21 days to develop a new habit, 21 days to become comfortable with a new routine.** Once a habit is established, it will be your friend for life. Promise yourself that you will make it a habit to say "Yes" to the things of God, and "No" to the rest. Make early lesson preparation a priority, and enjoy your new habit of a quiet, peaceful, confident spirit.

A habit is simply the way you usually do something that requires doing on a repeated basis. When you clean house. How you hang your clothes. What time you go to bed. How you spend Sunday afternoons. Habits dig themselves into the brain so that you don't even think about some tasks as you complete them for the umpteen millionth time.

Teaching children is not a weekly chore meant to add to your stress. Preparing for teaching in a habitual way—whatever method you choose—takes a lot of the tension out of the job. And you'll be a better teacher because of the habit.

My Choice

Of the five methods for early-in-the-week lesson preparation, the one I will commit to is:

_____

Let's look at some of the positive habits you already have. List **five positive habits** that relate to any part of your life.

1. _____

2. _____

3. _____

4. _____

5. _____

Take a look at how those habits relate to the things that are most important to you. List the **top five desires of your heart.** Will "Teach my kids to know and love God" fall somewhere on your list?

1. _____

2. _____

3. _____

4. _____

5. _____

The Mind of Christ

Delight yourself in the Lord and he will give you the desires of your heart.

Psalm 37:4

As you consider the desires that God has put in your heart, think about how teaching fits into God's plan for your life. Preparing your lesson gives you an opportunity to study his Word, to pray for the young people in your care and to expand your creative talents. Isn't that worth developing a new habit?

Build in some small rewards for your achievements along the way. Are you ready by Thursday the first week? Plan to do something special on Saturday. Did you feel more relaxed in class because you were prepared? Treat yourself to an afternoon nap.

Today's date: _____

I want to spend 21 days developing this new habit for teaching:

_____

21 days from now, I'll celebrate by:

_____

Make Your Path Straight

Now that you've determined to develop a new habit of starting your lesson prep early in the week, you need to clear the tracks of obstacles that might derail you. Remember—there's an enemy who loves chaos. But…

God is not a God of disorder but of peace

1 Corinthians 14:33

How many times have you wished you'd said "No" to something so that you could focus on what you really feel called to do? If your calling and priority is teaching children, learn to say "No" to other things that will keep you from doing the best job you can. "No" can be hard to say. Here's some help.

Sorry, but that's not something I do."
(Paul Newman's answer to those seeking autographs.)

I'm so glad you asked. But it just doesn't work for me right now.

How wonderful of you to ask. I'm so disappointed I must say no.

"I'm truly honored that you asked me, but this is a busy week (month, year, decade) for me and, unfortunately, I won't be able to fit it in."

I'd love to say yes, but I'm going to pass this time.

I've been praying about my priorities, and nothing is more important to me than teaching children about Jesus. I'd love to talk to you about helping in my class.

Practice these nice ways of saying "No" aloud in the shower. The folks in your family may think you've gone a little loopy, but out-loud practice is very empowering! You are a creative and committed person. Your name will always be the first to pop into the mind of someone looking for volunteers. Saying "No" to the good is saying "Yes" to the best: having the time and energy to be the teacher your class deserves.

Lord, there is never enough time. Help me do a little less a little better.

Think of the way each child in your class will impact others—for good or for evil. An hour richly invested in preparing your lesson may bring a child to faith in Jesus Christ. That child may influence thousands for many generations to come. Think of the loving moms and dads they will be, the grandmas and grandpas they will become. Some will be teachers, pastors, doctors. Maybe even president.

Children don't care how much you know until they know how much you care.

Someone just like *you* taught Billy Graham, Dwight Moody and Jimmy Carter. Writer and preacher Warren Wiersbe has said, "You are a Christian today because somebody cared. Now it's your turn." Whether you're a teacher because you eagerly volunteered or because you were reluctantly pressed into service, your loving touch can help change the lives of children. Put your ministry in God's hands; let him use you.

> **The Mind of Christ**
> If any of you lacks wisdom, he should ask God, who gives generously to all without finding fault, and it will be given to him.
> James 1:5

♡ ♡ ♡ ♡ ♡ ♡ ♡

Ready for Creativity

Being prepared to do a job means having the right tools. For a children's ministry worker, that means having lots and lots of things on hand, from basic classroom supplies to a special razzle-dazzle attention getting gadget. A few basics will keep you ready for a wide range of situations.

> **The Mind of Christ**
> A new command I give you: Love one another. As I have loved you, so you must love one another. By this all men will know that you are my disciples, if you love one another.
> John 13:34-35

Be bold! Become a children's ministry bag lady. Carry a cool tote bag. You can get one at any craft store for a nominal price and decorate it yourself—or have your kids help you do it. Then fill it with easy-to-find things that will make it possible for you to carry out your creative impulses without any last-minute panic.

Ten Fun Things to Carry in Your Tote
...and Why You Need Them

1 Puppet...   for story time

2 Bubbles...   create a game

3 Bright markers...   let children create

4 Stuffed animal...   have children tell the story from the mouth of the animal

5 Stickers...   rewards for cooperation

6 Small photo album with pictures of many children...   pray for children of the world

7 Bible story book...   divide a large class and let a parent read to one group while you work with another

8 Small puzzle or games...   for the really early arrival

9 CD or cassette of favorite children's praise songs...   when your music helper is sick

10 Swiss army knife...   can solve almost any emergency

You can create meaningful times with the surprises in your tote bag. These 10 items provide countless combinations of two, three or four that keep you prepared for anything. When might you dig into this bag?

• When you have more children than you planned for.

• When the sermon goes extra long.

• When the situation calls for you to punt.

Do those things ever happen to you?

> *Life is what thou makest it. So makest it FUN!*

Memorize? Who me? Yes, you.

Write out the verse for your class for the following Sunday on a small card.

☑ Carry it with you.

☑ Challenge your family to learn it with you.

☑ Ask a Christian co-worker or prayer partner to keep you accountable.

☑ Use these verses in your conversation.

☑ Make a cassette tape of your verses so you can review them during your commute.

> The Mind of Christ
>
> *I*nstead of saying,
> "I'm so busy..." "I've always been
> a procrastinator..."
> "I can just wing it this week..."
> Say with the Apostle Paul,
> "I can do everything through him
> who gives me strength."
> Philippians 4:13

Lesson Planner

The main passage:

_____

The main point:

_____

How kids will know God better because of this lesson:

_____

Things I need:

Gather from home   Beg, borrow or deal!

_____   _____

_____   _____

Planning my teaching time:

From (starting time) to (finish)   We'll do this:

1. _____ /_____   _____

2. _____ /_____   _____

3. _____ /_____   _____

4. _____ /_____   _____

5. _____ /_____   _____

Praying for my kids this week:

Name   Request

_____   _____

_____   _____

_____   _____

_____   _____

4 Cooties, Cliques
and other Delightful
Realities
about Kids

Joan circulated among her preschoolers as they colored their arks in preparation for the morning's lesson about Noah.

Some were floating little boats in a dishpan of water. Others were matching up the plastic animals two by two. All were intent on their projects—except Timmy. He zoomed around the room pretending to be an airplane, yanked Chelsea's ponytail, then climbed up on the supply cabinet and announced he could fly.

Joan caught him just as he jumped and gathered him into her arms. "Timmy, this just isn't like you. You're usually such a good helper in class. Who's this little goofus I see today?"

To which Timmy replied, "I'm not a little goofus. My grandma thinks I'm precious."

This is the delightful reality about children. They can be "goofuses" and precious all in the same moment. **Our challenge as teachers is to understand how God has created his precious children to learn and develop.** We can learn to recognize distinct phases that children typically pass through on their journey from infancy to adulthood. Being informed about such tricky matters as "cooties" and cliques will help you anticipate, adapt, innovate and overcome!

It doesn't take many weeks in the classroom to discover that God blesses each child with a different set of gifts. Which child loves to sing, moves in time to the music and drives you crazy tapping rhythms on the craft table? Is there **a child who loves to dress up** and roleplay and insists on touching everything? Does one always retreat to a quiet corner rather than join in the class activities? These children are not trying to make your life difficult. They're just being the way God created them to be!

Let's look at some of the ways God has gifted his children. Howard Gardner, a professor of education at the Harvard Graduate School of Education, has identified eight different intelligences. These "multiple intelligences" explain how God created us to respond individually in different ways to different kinds of content, such as language, music, nature or other people. As you read these descriptions, think about children you know and teach. Which gifts do the children in your class exhibit?

We have different gifts, according to the grace given us.
Romans 12:6

Every child possesses all eight gifts, but operates most comfortably with the dominant one or two. Each student's learning style will consist of a different combination of these gifts. Children learn best when classroom activities appeal to their dominant intelligence. Therefore the wise teacher includes activities that appeal to each learning style.

Choose teaching material that provides you a smorgasbord of activities so you'll be sure to teach each child in your class effectively. And be aware that you're most likely to choose activities that best suit your own learning style! Be careful not to fall into the trap of doing what's most comfortable for you each week. Teach with your kids in mind.

Remember: each child is created in the image of God, according to God's perfect plan. You become a mentor and faith-friend as you creatively seek to meet each child's needs and help in the learning process.

Each child is created in the IMAGE of God, according to God's PERFECT plan.

8 Gifts for  Learning

Kids in my class who demonstrate this intelligence

LINGUISTIC (word gift)

Child: learns by seeing and hearing words

Teacher: provide books, paper, tape recorder

LOGICAL-MATHEMATICAL (logic gift)

Child: learns by looking for abstract patterns

Teacher: provide games, puzzles, items children can manipulate

SPATIAL (picture gift)

Child: learns by pictures, colors, images

Teacher: provide art supplies, picture books, video

BODILY-KINESTHETIC (body gift)

Child: learns by moving, touching, manipulating

Teacher: provide roleplaying and physical activities

MUSICAL (music gift)

Child: learns through melody and rhythm

Teacher: provide singing, playing musical instruments

INTERPERSONAL (people gift)

Child: learns by cooperating with others

Teacher: provide social interaction

INTRAPERSONAL (self-awareness gift)

Child: learns best when left alone

Teacher: provide a private space

NATURALIST (classifying gift)

Child: learns by classifying

Teacher: provide outdoor activities

Negotiate the Pitfalls

Appreciating the variety of learning styles that God gives children helps us avoid assumptions that lead to common pitfalls. Not only do children learn in different ways, they also develop at different rates. Family and health issues may alter a child's development. An only child may be very comfortable with adults and have verbal skills well beyond his or her years. A youngest child may be encouraged at home to continue in the "baby mode"—an attitude which often results in delayed verbal skills. It's a challenge to have two such opposite children in the same class.

Children who are labeled "difficult" are often reacting to stresses in the home or experiencing the world in a different way because of how God created them. Those children need you to see them through God's eyes. Look beyond the behavior to the heart of the matter. Children who struggle with behavioral issues can be a drain on your energy. But each one is a precious child of God who needs your teaching and your attention, perhaps more than any other in your class.

Common Pitfalls

#1
Assuming all children learn in the same way

#2
Assuming all children enjoy the same activities

#3
Assuming all children develop at the same rate

#4
Assuming a child is "difficult"

Just as Jesus grew in wisdom (mentally and emotionally) and stature (physically), and in favor with God (spiritually) and man (socially), **each of the children in your class will grow according to God's plan.** Ask God to help you be sensitive and responsive to your children's needs.

♡ ♡ ♡ ♡ ♡ ♡ ♡

What to Expect

God has built into children a pattern for development. Understanding what's typical of each age and stage of development gives you the insights you need to create a learning environment where kids can thrive in their mental, physical, spiritual and social growth. Because each child is growing and developing at a different rate, expect to have children in your class who are behind or beyond a typical development schedule. Don't try to rush or restrain those whose abilities differ from others. Give kids the freedom to be who God made them and to develop at their own God-given pace.

And Jesus grew in wisdom and stature, and in favor with God and men.
Luke 2:52

PRESCHOOL

Mentally, preschoolers

- Have short attention spans
- Ask many questions
- Are learning language rapidly
- Fear the unfamiliar
- Feel important when you ask them to help
- Learn through their senses
- Are curious
- Have active imaginations
- Think very concretely
- Have intense emotions

Socially, preschoolers

- Are self-centered
- Are learning to take turns
- Like to try new things
- Enjoy playing side by side, sometimes share a task
- Will laugh one minute, cry the next

Spiritually, preschoolers

- Can understand that Jesus loves them
- Are filled with wonder
- Love to be read Bible stories
- Accept what they are told
- Begin to see the difference between right and wrong
- Can experience worship

Physically, preschoolers

- Are active, love to run and jump
- Are developing their large muscles
- Use the floor, not the table
- Are growing rapidly
- Have boundless energy
- Tire easily
- Are developing fine motor skills

To teach 3 year-olds effectively

- Involve all five senses in class activities
- Provide opportunities to explore
- Help children feel comfortable when parents leave
- Give all children a chance to help
- Provide concrete experiences and examples
- Use clear, simple words; avoid clichés and symbolism
- Include active times for large muscle movement
- Encourage them to do things for themselves
- Always teach with your Bible open
- Use simple songs about Jesus
- Tell Bible stories with great enthusiasm and vocal expression
- Ask questions that begin, "I wonder…"
- Move them through transitions by giving clues about what happens next
- Emphasize how much God loves them
- Provide times of worship
- Encourage sharing
- Make suggestions for group play

☼ **Little ones see the world as a very big place.** Get down on their level. Crawl around your classroom on your knees to see how it looks from their perspective. It's frustrating not to be able to see over tables and counters. Provide kid-sized chairs, tables, games. When you teach, don't be a giant! Sit with them on a low chair or on the floor so you can look them in the eye.

☼ **Little ones need to feel in control of their environment.** They like to take things apart and put them back together. Stack up blocks for them to knock over. Provide puzzles, blocks, and Legos that they can manage. Provide a rubber mallet to drive golf tees into Styrofoam packing material. Give them an appliance box to make their own private space. What looks like a mess to us is just part of the discovery process to them.

☼ **Little ones are curious and observant.** What looks ordinary to us is full of wonder to a young child. Provide an environment where they can explore God's fascinating world to their heart's content. Set out flashlights and magnifying glasses. Take a 36-inch hike: give each child 36-inch length of string to place in a circle on the ground. Ask what they can find in the circle. Set up a "science table" in your classroom. Invite children to bring in rocks, shells, acorns and leaves.

☼ **Little ones love to use their senses: sight, sound, touch, taste, smell.** This is their favorite way to learn. Bake cookies (smell and taste). Fingerpaint (touch). Act out the music (sound and movement). Play "I spy" with shapes and colors in your classroom (sight).

☼ **Little ones experience emotions they don't understand.** Help them learn the vocabulary for the feelings they have. Say, "you are feeling frustrated because you can't find your shoes." Look at pictures in magazines, identifying feelings expressed on faces. Ask them to tell you about times they were happy, sad, angry.

☼ **Little ones need to use their imaginations.** They often have trouble sorting out what is real and what isn't. Preschoolers love to pretend; by school age they begin to realize that there is a logical explanation for everything. Encourage children to pretend with dolls and puppets.

YOUNGER ELEMENTARY

Mentally, younger elementary kids

- Live in the present
- Learn best from creative activities
- Love to learn, explore, investigate
- Think concretely; do not interpret symbols
- Are growing phenomenally in language skills
- Can begin to sort out fact from fantasy

Physically, younger elementary kids

- Are growing slowly, sporadically
- Have bursts of energy
- Have trouble sitting still
- Tire easily

Spiritually, younger elementary kids

- Enjoy learning at church
- Are open to learning about God
- Find it difficult to express feelings
- Pray easily if encouraged
- Accept what authority figures tell them

Socially, younger elementary kids

- Love to have a best friend, but change friends often
- Mimic the adults in their lives
- Are especially loyal to teachers
- Have developed a sense of right and wrong
- Enjoy working in groups

To teach younger elementary kids effectively

- Treat each child as a unique individual
- Provide activities for experimenting and exploring
- Make application to the here and now
- Plan something active for each lesson
- Use emerging reading, writing, counting skills
- Plan hands-on art and craft activities
- Avoid detail work
- Use only the simplest symbolism
- Explain what is fact and what is fantasy
- Provide roleplay experiences and group projects
- Make prayer and worship a natural part of the time together
- Be worthy of their respect and admiration

☼ **Younger elementary kids really believe the other sex has cooties!** Avoid activities that require kids of the opposite sex to hold hands. Sometimes children will hold hands for an activity on their own, but never force the issue.

☼ **Younger elementary kids believe everything you tell them.** Sarcasm is far above their level of understanding. Avoid speaking sarcastically at all cost, even in humor. Speak literally since they understand literally.

☼ **Younger elementary kids are growing in autonomy.** They're beginning to find out who they are and what they like. Provide kids with choices to help them grow in this arena. Would they like an apple or a banana for snack? Would they prefer to be an actor or part of the audience this time?

☼ **Younger elementary kids love to help!** Helping the teacher or any other person in authority gives them a huge boost of self-confidence. Give every child a chance to help out. Send them on special errands for you. Provide classroom jobs that the kids can take turns accomplishing.

☼ **Younger elementary kids are active, active, active!** Don't expect these youngsters to sit still for more than five minutes at the most. Always provide some sort of action that they can do. Utilize their energy using both fine-motor and gross-motor activities in the context of your lessons. Do you have a long story to tell? Figure out movements that they can do to participate in the story. Have them make sounds and noises during certain parts of the story. They can "make" an object from the story using their bodies. Use their activity to your benefit; don't make it your detriment.

OLDER ELEMENTARY

Mentally, older elementary kids

- Are curious; ask lots of questions
- Love to reason and discuss
- Begin to develop longer attention spans
- Can memorize and recite
- Are developing self-confidence
- Can think abstractly
- Have a more mature sense of time and space
- Are aware that adults are not always right
- Want to make their own decisions

Physically, younger elementary kids

- Grow steadily
- Enjoy being active
- Want to participate rather then watch
- Mature at different rates
- Are noisy and love to compete
- Become aware of the opposite sex

Spiritually, younger elementary kids

- Begin to ask questions about Christianity
- Evaluate different points of view
- Enjoy participating in worship
- Can learn to apply Christian truth to their own moral behavior
- Like to share and participate in church activities
- Can express spiritual thoughts in spoken and written word

Socially, younger elementary kids

- Learn better ways to make and keep friends
- Are interested in cultures around the world
- Have strong feelings about right and wrong
- Need to belong to a peer group
- Are learning to relate to peers of both sexes
- Are becoming more responsible and dependable
- Tend to form cliques

To teach older elementary kids effectively

- Provide challenging activities
- Offer times to think, reason, solve problems
- Suggest reading and writing activities
- Provide an atmosphere of acceptance and trust
- Supply a variety of creative activities
- Allow time for movement and games
- Avoid comparison and competition between boys and girls
- Provide worship and fellowship experiences for both sexes
- Encourage students to read the Bible and apply it to their behavior
- Bring in adult role models who are committed to serving God
- Help them understand the plan of salvation
- Guide them in expressing their own faith

☼ **Older elementary kids need more freedom to experience success and failure for themselves.** Learning to accept and grow from failure is a key part of growing up. Keep track of kids' accomplishments on a regular basis. Break down "failures" into smaller chunks so kids can feel good about what they've learned and analyze what they need to move on toward success.

☼ **Older elementary kids learn to see God everywhere. They understand that God is real, eternal and supremely powerful.** They know that God cares for them and acts on their behalf. Help kids develop a consistent prayer life. Encourage them to call on God when struggles arise at home, on the playing field or in the food court at the mall.

☼ **Older elementary kids need a safe place to express their feelings of protest.** Learning how to integrate good and bad feelings is an essential process for older kids. Allowing kids the opportunity to "vent" is a healthy first step in eliminating the power struggle that often erupts between kids and those in authority. Remain calm and firm in your decisions, but allow for the heated responses that are sure to follow.

☼ **Older elementary kids learn through experience how to reconcile with others.** Reality is a good teacher. Anger, guilt or alienation will not bring back a good friend. Kids will use trial and error to work out problems in relationships. Be available to make suggestions and broaden perspectives, but let kids work things out for themselves.

☼ **Older elementary kids come to see themselves as imperfect people in an imperfect world.** As kids mature and form a more objective view of reality, they become increasingly aware of their own flaws. God's unconditional love becomes more important to them. They need role models who offer grace and forgiveness.

Faith Steps

Why do we invest so much time and energy in children's ministry? Because we know we are helping to form disciples, helping children to know God, showing them how God can transform their lives and relationships.

A child's belief system develops from several bases including relationships, personal experience and knowledge. Wisely constructed lessons unfold the person of God through all these avenues in order to place kids in a position where they're ready to allow God to enter their lives with his transforming power. **A discerning teacher senses when the Holy Spirit has prepared a child's heart,** offers the simple truth of the Gospel, and allows a child to respond.

> We pray this in order that you may live a life worthy of the Lord and may please him in every way: bearing fruit in every good work, growing in the knowledge of God.
>
> Colossians 1:10

As you learn to know and love your students, you will see the stages of their developing faith. You may see expressions of faith that surprise and delight you. Some children may have insights that seem beyond their years. Remember, the Holy Spirit is at work in these children, preparing them to be Christ's disciples.

Preschoolers live in a very concrete world. Their lives are a here-and-now, touch-and-feel experience. Express the truth of each lesson in simple, concrete language appropriate to a preschooler's understanding of God and how God relates to his people.

- *God is always with us.*
- *God helps us care for others.*
- *God's people serve together.*

Preschoolers grow to understand basic truths that form the foundations of their faith.

- *I am precious to God.*
- *God's people care for me.*
- *I can do what pleases God.*

As children grow into the elementary years, they're ready to make personal decisions about their faith. As you learn to know and love your students, you may find them ready to make a commitment to Christ. How will you lead them in this important step of faith?

If you sense that a child is ready to open his or her life to God, speak simply and directly. "Do you know how much God loves you, Eric? Do you know that God wants to make you his special child and welcome you into his family?" Use these Scriptures to explain God's plan of salvation. You may want to read them from the Bible, or explain the truth in children's language.

Psalm 139:13–16:
God loved you even before you were born.
He knows all about you and has a wonderful plan for your life.

1 John 1:9–10:
No one is perfect enough for God. We all sin and mess up.

John 3:16:
God sent Jesus to pay for the sins of the whole world—
including yours! Jesus wants to be your Savior.
Would you like to pray to accept him?

1 John 3:1
God has given you a wonderful gift—he's made you his child!

Children approach God with very different levels of spiritual maturity and understanding. Their first expression of faith won't make them theological experts! Faith development is a lifelong process. Encourage children to open their lives to God's love and transforming power. Remember, every step toward God is a good one.

You can tell the whole Gospel story
in just eight words:

God loves.

We sin.

Jesus saves.

You choose.

Guide **younger elementary kids** to make connections between what God is and what God wants us to be. Express the truth of each lesson in a way that builds this bridge.

- *God has a plan; he can use me.*
- *Jesus loves everyone; I can love people who are different.*
- *God is faithful to me; I can be faithful to God.*

In response to these truths, **younger elementary kids** begin to make connections to their own lives.

- *I know what God is like.*
- *I can be like God in the way I treat others.*
- *What is important to God should be important to me.*

Older elementary children can understand the link between what God is and what he helps us to be. They are able to make choices to be Christlike. Express the truth of a lesson in a way that challenges the students to choose a life of discipleship.

- *Because God is the only true God, I worship and obey him.*
- *Because God is a God of peace, I can take the first step to end an argument.*
- *Because Jesus accepted God's will, I can obey God even when it's hard.*

Older elementary kids can personalize their responses.

- *God shows himself to me in my everyday life.*
- *I can show other people what God is like by being like him.*
- *I want to serve God with my whole life.*

The *most* delightful reality about children is that God wants them in his family. Perhaps the greatest joy and privilege a teacher has is praying for each child in the class. One of the most effective ways to pray is to pray Scripture, personalizing it for each child. We can be certain we are praying in God's will when we pray God's Word.

Pray the words of SCRIPTURE for each child in your class:

Create in _____ a clean heart, O God, and renew a steadfast spirit within him/her.

Psalm 51:10

Deliver _____ from the evil one.

Matthew 6:13

I pray that out of your glorious riches, you may strengthen _____ with power through the Holy Spirit in his/her inner being, so that you may dwell in his/her heart through faith. And I pray that _____, being rooted and established in love, may have power, together with all the saints, to grasp how wide and long and high and deep is your love, and to know that this love surpasses knowledge—that _____ may be filled to the measure of all your fullness.

Ephesians 3:16–19

Then pray for yourself:

May the words of my mouth and the meditation of my heart be pleasing in your sight, O Lord, my Rock and my Redeemer.

Psalm 19:14

AMEN.

5

The Marvels of Motivation

I've heard that story already."

"Coloring? Again?"

"This looks boring."

Words to make a teacher's heart sink. Unfortunately, we've all heard them. Our kids' lives roll along at an incredible pace. See if you can take in the number of images per second crammed into TV commercials aimed at kids. Or watch the dizzying pace of games in a video arcade. All this mind-boggling excitement draws kids like flies to a feast.

Are we in the church capable of competing with what the media has to offer? You bet! **We can be "high touch" in a "high tech" world.** We can interact on a caring level that kids in a "point and click" environment hunger for. We can offer joy that doesn't fade with the credits. We can go beyond the virtual to the absolutely real.

It's time for the church to reclaim its children! How?

Well, let's start with one little letter: "**I**."

I can make my children's ministry classroom fun!

I can create an atmosphere where the children will long to be.

I can volunteer my time and make a difference—if only in one child's life.

I can show parents and children alike that knowing and loving God is neither a chore nor a bore, but an exciting privilege.

Since you're reading this book, you've obviously made that important and life-changing decision to give of yourself to children. One of the realities about kids is that they don't always give back the way you wish they would. So how do you motivate them? How do you create a sense of anticipation so they can't wait to come to church?"

Take heart. You *can* motivate your kids. This chapter will give you eight keys to motivation that you can use in your class next week.

Start with a great foundation. Choose children's ministry materials that incorporate the key principles of motivation. Insist on a curriculum that

- is child-friendly and relational
- is based on sound principles of child development
- is richly creative in its approach to Bible study
- doesn't rush children through the Bible, but allows them to gain deep understanding so they have time to understand how to live out Bible truth
- lets children experience the joy of group prayer and of witnessing God at work through their prayers
- relies less on reading and writing and more on learning techniques that use all the senses
- gives children a sense of ownership
- makes Bible memory fun with exciting, meaningful songs
- puts choices at your fingertips that appeal to each child
- is full of energetic, positive language
- is fun and full of novelty without sacrificing meaty Bible content
- teaches children not just about God, but to know God
- builds in time to pause for review and celebration of what kids have learned and how they've grown

Resources based in these motivating factors will be your ally. Material that's predictable and heavily reliant on reading and information transfer will make your job harder. If you're using Godprints curriculum, you've seen how all these marvels of motivation are carefully integrated into each lesson.

Children have a natural hunger to know their Creator. When they're allowed to explore that relationship in child-friendly ways, they feel empowered and motivated. Ellie is a perfect example.

Kids are natural LEARNERS

*E*llie was a second grader from a solid family at the core of the church. Yet when it was time for Sunday school, Ellie managed to be running around the church foyer or scooting up the tree outside the front door. Once captured and delivered to her teacher, Ellie's head hung low and she scowled. She entered the classroom with a ritual warning: "I'm not going to read anything today." Then she would tuck herself away in a cubbyhole between two cabinets in the classroom.

Ellie was a bright child. She was in a gifted program for math. She was inquisitive, energetic and enthusiastic about many things. Just not Sunday school. Why? Because in Sunday school, she was expected to read, and she wasn't good at reading. Ellie, like all other children, was a natural learner. But the Sunday school curriculum her church used expected second graders to be able to read a printed script of the Bible story nearly every week. Ellie wasn't good at that. She was good at acting out a part. She was good at creating parts and putting on an imaginary radio script with a partner who did the writing. She was good at turning the story into a dynamic activity, planning sound effects and directing dramatic action. But she wasn't good at reading. So she was de-motivated to come to Sunday school.

Children have a built-in drive to master new challenges.

How else would a six month old learn to sit up, or a nine month old learn to crawl or a one year old learn to walk? Children learn to talk, to control their bodies in coordinated movements, to count, to read, to kick a soccer ball. God created children so that they want to grow and learn. Conquering new challenges brings satisfaction and builds self-esteem.

All children are motivated to learn until we teach them differently. Motivating children to learn during a children's ministry program is no different than motivating them in any other arena. It comes down to understanding what already motivates them and making wise use of that. For teachers in the church, it's *motivation to learn* that is critical, not merely motivation to follow rules, to conform, to keep order in the classroom.

Key 1: Make an Emotional Connection

If you want kids to be motivated and eager to learn, you need to make an emotional connection. The part of the brain that governs emotion can either boost learning or shut it down. **Children need good reasons to do what you're asking them to do, a reason that matters to them personally.** It might be pride in an accomplishment, the pleasure of an activity, the satisfaction of completing a challenging task or the excitement of investigating something new. If that emotional, personal connection is missing, kids won't be motivated to learn through the activity you have planned. On the flip side is the power of negative emotion.

Key 2: Remove Fear

Fear or threat turns off the learning switch. Instead, children focus on making it through the painful time—even defending themselves if necessary.

Even church, a place filled with people who love God and want the best for his children, can be a threatening place for children. Ellie felt threatened at church. Josh, whose teacher told him he wasn't allowed to fidget with his toy car during Sunday school, felt threatened. Luke, whose body did not allow him to sit still for more than four minutes at a time, felt threatened by teachers who told him he must sit quietly in the circle for the Bible story.

When the emotional part of the brain feels threatened, the "fight or flight" response takes over. Nothing will persuade Ellie to try to read. Nothing will make Josh forget about the car that was taken away from him and pay attention to prayer circle. Nothing can force Luke to learn the details of the Bible story if he's not allowed to move his body around.

Key 3: **Challenge**

When there's a sense of emotional connection and safety, what the child needs next is a challenge. **Human brains are created by God to respond to challenge, especially if there is a reasonable chance of success.** Kids respond to games in the children's ministry classroom because games bring a challenge to succeed. For a child like Luke, a Bible story presented in an active game format will result in more learning than if he's forced to keep himself still. He'll think, "Wow! This is something I can do. I wish the Bible story were like this every week."

Key 4: **Choice**

Choice plays a *huge* role in motivation. **Selfdetermination is a God-given characteristic of the human race.** Of course, we all need to do what we're told. But from time to time, the opportunity to make a choice encourages children and adults alike to invest themselves in what they've chosen.

Let children choose what character they'll play as they act out the Bible story. Let them choose from art supplies you've set out for a project. Let them choose among life application activities that appeal to different learning styles. You'll be amazed at how kids are willing to invest in the choices they make.

Key 5: **Emotional Payoff**

Emotional connection leads kids to respond to challenge, and challenge is meaningful only if there is a "payoff." What will the kids get out of it? If they do what you want them to do, what's in it for them? Answering this question leads some teachers to the use of positive reward systems, which can motivate students who have difficulty motivating themselves. **Positive reward systems provide a reward for good choices the kids make.** If you can say your memory verse, you earn points toward going to camp. If you finish the handout on time, you get to be the assistant teacher for a day. As long as kids clearly understand the expectations, positive reward systems can be simple and effective.

Kids who are internally motivated need fewer rewards. Use external rewards sparsely and wisely. As often as you can, let the reward be the joy of learning something new, the awareness of new growth, and the glow of success in meeting a challenge.

Key 6: Achievable Expectations

Set expectations that are reasonable and achievable for the kids in your class. For instance, don't expect a kindergartner to sit as long as a third grader. Understand and anticipate your kids' attention spans, and gear activities to fit within them.

While reward systems may work to solve short-term problems, real learning happens when the reward comes from within the child—the self-esteem and satisfaction that come with a completed task. That means creating challenges that children can actually master. The "unmotivated" children in your classroom perhaps have had fewer experiences of success in mastering something new. A pattern of failure discourages them from trying. It's so important to give children experiences of success that help them move forward with their God-given drive to learn.

The Motivation Test

Classrooms with motivated learners have these characteristics:

- ☑ Strong commitment to the children
- ☑ A teacher who sees things from a child's point of view
- ☑ Structure and consistency
- ☑ Carefully designed challenges
- ☑ Choices
- ☑ Opportunities for independent learning
- ☑ More than one way to show what you've learned
- ☑ Humor and fun

Key 7: Establish Caring Relationships

It's as simple as this: kids who love you want to please you. Experiences of success have as much to do with relationships as with mastering content. When children work hard to understand a new Bible truth and integrate it into their lives, they need to be encouraged and affirmed both by children's ministry leaders at church and by parents at home. **Notice and comment on small steps of progress.** It's easy for little celebrations to be overlooked because, in an adult's eyes, the achievement isn't all that significant. Express your sincere love for children in winsome ways. Smile with your voice and your eyes as well as your mouth. Punctuate your words of encouragement with a caring touch on a child's shoulder or elbow. Ask God to set you aglow with his love.

This relational dimension of teaching matters enormously. Take time to celebrate answered prayer, to shout hooray after a Bible review game that shows how much kids have learned, to give a pat on the back to a child who's not having a good day. Warm, positive relationships can provide the emotional connection that starts the learning chain.

Key 6: Anticipation

Curiosity. Something out of the ordinary. That millisecond flash when you make eye contact and know you've caught a child's attention. **You can help build the emotional connection needed for learning by creating mystery, excitement and anticipation about what is to come.** You've caught their attention and they're eager to learn.

You can build a VOLCANO of anticipation with these easy ideas.

1. CHOOSE YOUR WORDS. Don't just relay information. Sound excited. Use relational words.

- "Wait until you get here next week! You won't believe it!"

- "I've been working really hard on something special for us to do later on!"

- "You will be here next week, won't you? You won't want to miss what we're going to do!"

2. PLAN EVENTS FOR KIDS TO LOOK FORWARD TO. This might be a special class party, an open house for parents, a service project or a special guest in the classroom. For great examples of how to plan a quick and easy event, check out Celebration FUNday—the last lesson of each quarter in

Godprints curriculum. Each week, for three or four weeks, before a "big event" occurs, put up a decorated, kid-friendly sign near the doorway. Try messages such as:

- Don't miss the BIG EVENT!
- You won't believe your eyes! See it live Sunday, December 12!
- You've waited 8 years for something like this! Bring a friend!

3. PROJECTS THAT BUILD OWNERSHIP IN THE KIDS. Over a period of a few weeks, have the kids work on a major project. Once the project is finished, use it as part of a larger project or production. For example, build a tissue paper and chicken wire cross and use it as part of your Easter service. Allow the kids to help plan and prepare for the special project. Let the anticipation build, then watch how kids delight in taking ownership in part of the Easter service.

4. BREAK OUT OF THE ORDINARY. PLAN SURPRISES. Make your children's ministry program unpredictable. Kids may not know exactly when this week's surprise will happen or what it will be, but they will begin to anticipate something fun happening each week.

- Use a new or special puppet to introduce a story or activity.
- Bring in a "Bible character"—a volunteer dressed up in bathrobe and sandals—to tell your Bible story. Have the person pop into your room unannounced and address the kids directly.
- If you teach in a space that you are free to decorate, change the decorations in your room frequently. Kids will come running in to see what's new. Tease them with the decoration; let them speculate what the black crepe paper on the bulletin board might mean.
- Surprise kids with new gel pens.
- Do a food surprise. Hide the strawberries or donut holes under a paper bag and let kids guess what you've brought.
- Take kids on a mini-service project outside the classroom. Have them make treat bags for preschoolers or visit an adult classroom to share their memory verse song.

Use teaching material that gives you lots of imaginative choices! You'll be a step ahead of the game if you do!

Ellie's Happy Ending

Pemember Ellie? Fast forward a few weeks. Her teacher quickly learned not to ask Ellie to read. In fact, she did away with any required reading for any of the kids in the class. She began a new approach to teaching.

One day Ellie dragged herself into the room, stopped in her tracks and looked around. "What is this?" she asked. "A game room?"

In one corner was a Bible story jigsaw puzzle. On another table was a Bible review board game. Other children were busy at both tasks. The main part of the room featured a large stuffed lamb, a table full of foreign coins, and a big sign that said, "Get your temple offering here!"

The lesson for the day: Jesus cleansing the temple. Ellie was suspicious.

"Sunday school can be fun," the teacher said.

"Not usually," was Ellie's response.

"Why not?" The teacher wondered, as Ellie moved toward the table and began to pick up the foreign coins and examine them. Why should any child ever feel that way about Sunday school?

Children's ministry is not just about transferring information about the Bible from the teacher's head to the children's heads. It's about touching their hearts, prompting them to act on their natural desire to learn. Motivating children to be fully engaged with the lesson means looking at things from their perspective. Take yourself out of the teacher's big chair and mentally sit in one of those little blue plastic chairs made for little bottoms. What does your class look like from there? What can you do to make it more interesting—to build the emotional connection that sparks a challenge and leads to a payoff of successful learning?

Here are some simple ideas:

● **Dress as a character in your story.** Don't act as yourself at all! Stay in character the entire time you're with your kids—or better yet, the entire time you're at church. Use an accent!

● **Participate in an activity yourself.** If the kids are creating palaces using all sorts of edibles, you make a palace too. If the kids are painting their feet to create multi-colored footprints, paint yours too. This builds an important relational bridge. Interact and get to know the kids on a deeper level while you're working together.

● **Decorate your room**! Use the themes in your stories for decorating ideas. For example, decorate your room as the desert when studying the Israelites wandering, the inside of a whale's belly for Jonah's story, the canopy of a rainforest for Zacchaeus! This works especially well if you use a curriculum that features the same Bible story for two weeks or more.

● **Sparkle with enthusiasm.** If you are motivated about something, your kids will naturally become motivated. Motivation—both positive and negative—rubs off and sticks to anyone who happens to be nearby!

Key 9: Multi-Aging and Motivation

Kindergartners and fourth graders are thoroughly different. How can you possibly put them in a class together and expect them to learn anything?

Are they really so different? It's true that the older child will have higher level verbal and cognitive abilities, better fine motor skills, stronger physical abilities. No one expects the five year old and the nine year old to "perform" identically in the classroom. But they can benefit from being together. They both need relationships. They both need meaningful participation in the lesson. They both have needs that being with the other child can meet.

When older children are mixed with younger children, the older ones instinctively know they can set an example. Many will intuitively pair up with a younger child who needs help with a project or reading instructions. Even if they need a teacher's encouragement to partner with a younger child, the older child will be quick to jump into the role of mentor. The older child is looking for opportunities to show leadership and demonstrate accomplishments. That's a natural part of the way kids develop. A multi-age classroom allows older kids—even those whose verbal abilities are less than stellar—to be looked up to, to do something that matters, to serve in a meaningful way. They thrive on that.

The younger child likes the attention of the older child. The kindergartner likes the grown-up feeling of working on a project with a fourth grader. Being paired with an older child is cool! The younger child rises to the challenge to keep pace and succeed together.

Some fourth graders might struggle with reading and math, while a few kindergartners and first graders will jump right into the academic scene. A younger child who has a lot of contact with adults may have a better vocabulary than an older child who spends most of his time with peers. **A multi-age classroom recognizes that all six year olds are not alike,** all eight year olds are not alike, all ten year olds are not alike. Each child develops at an individual pace. A multi-age classroom allows for wide differences in development without making a child feel out of place because abilities lag behind other children the same age. This is a natural environment for success.

If Ellie had been in a class where there were other children who didn't read well, she might have developed a different attitude about Sunday school. When she was paired with a child who was a good reader, Ellie blossomed. The pressure was off. She could do what she was good at, while Michael did what he was good at. Both succeeded, and the presentation they created together was something they were both proud of. Ellie was motivated to participate. Learning happened.

The Classroom

Advantages of a Multi-Age Classroom:

☑ Peer tutoring. Allowing kids who have "got it" to help those who need a little coaching.

☑ Older kids become the teacher's helpers…and we always need help!

☑ Older kids practice patience.

☑ Younger kids have someone to look up to.

☑ Younger kids love the attention the older ones give them.

☑ Older kids often feel "grown up" because of the responsibilities they're given.

☑ Grouping works wonderfully.

☑ Caring instincts develop.

☑ All kids are more willing to try things that look "too hard" or seem "too silly."

Multi-aging can be done on a small scale or a large scale. It's possible to put elementary age kids of all ages together; plan activities that make use of a whole spectrum of abilities, and **celebrate everyone's success.** You can even put kids and adults together and enjoy spectacular results in learning while also building important relationships. Multi-aging may be as simple as putting kids in three different grades together, rather than having every grade in a separate room. Within that three-year span of ages will be a wide spectrum of abilities. The six year old who is not quite like most other six year olds suddenly doesn't stand out. She blends into the range of abilities in the classroom and experiences success and affirmation.

The Wonderful, Marvelous, Very Good Feeling of Success

The feeling of success is one of the greatest gifts we can give others. Your position as a teacher provides you an opportunity to touch the lives of children—be it one child or twenty. The power of your words and actions on those students can be life changing.

James is a 15-year-old eighth grader. It's not that James is not a talented student. If the truth were known, he could probably have been the best student in his class. However, James is not motivated at school. He arrives on time, leaves on time, takes exactly 29 minutes for lunch every day and doesn't disturb the other students—when he's at school, that is. Most of the time he's truant. When he's at school, he refuses to do any work whatsoever. For someone who has tremendous potential, James seems content in his lack of effort. Why?

> *Encourage one another and build each other up, just as in fact you are doing.*
> 1 Thessalonians 5:11

In his 15 years of life, James has heard only a few positive remarks from his teachers. One was when he started kindergarten—the first time he started that is, and before his reputation preceded him. "We're glad you're here, James." Another was upon receiving his promotion out of the sixth grade—after a second try. "Well, you finally made it, James. Way to go."

James doesn't feel successful A few heart-felt compliments about his effort would jump-start James onto the motivational highway of hard work.

There's another James to meet—Jimmy. Jimmy has Down's syndrome. Jimmy's 19 and just about to graduate from high school. His mother tells everyone she meets, "My Jim's about to graduate! I'm so proud of my senior!" Jimmy's been the manager of the varsity football squad for the past three years and is one of the more popular kids on the team. During his junior year, Jimmy won a third place debate ribbon for his speech entitled "We're Just Like You: How to Befriend Kids with Special Needs." Jimmy sings in the men's choir at church, volunteers in the toddler room every second Sunday, and works part-time at the local zoo. Next year he'll work there full-time, apprenticing under the head-keeper for small mammals. **Jimmy not only feels successful, he knows he's successful.**

Affirmation and encouragement are great building blocks for success. Words are simple gifts to give, but they can make a world of difference to a child. Plan activities that set your kids up to succeed. Don't ask a three year old to construct a house with glue and toothpicks! Use lesson materials that give you options that are both creative and age-appropriate.

Early on, our first James met with failure. Perhaps he was not emotionally or physically mature enough to enter kindergarten. Perhaps he had a teacher who expected too much from him. But somewhere in that first year of school, James learned that he "couldn't do it." Instead of changing the situation so that James could succeed, perhaps someone kept telling him, "Try harder." (He was trying his hardest.) "You can't do that. You're too stupid." (Yes, it's actually been said.)

And Jimmy? Jimmy could have been written off. His parents could have said, "He has developmental difficulties. He'll never amount to anything." But Jimmy's family found where Jimmy could be successful. They capitalized on his successes, and that bred more success. Jimmy didn't hear, "You can't." He heard, "You can."

Affirmation, encouragement, accomplishment—these can produce the feeling of success in your students. **Be a cheerleader for your kids!** Let them know that you believe in them, God believes in them, and they can believe in themselves.

6 Sunday School in a Box–Or Not

*J*ackie approached the presenter after a workshop on the importance of building a creative learning environment for children.

During the workshop, teachers enjoyed a video tour of some of the most creative and extravagant children's ministry facilities in the world. With discouragement written all over her face, Jackie proceeded to paint a visual picture of the seven by ten-foot room she had to teach Sunday school in each week. The room was in the musty church basement and doubled as storage space. The presenter's first impulse was to tell Jackie to resign. Then he smiled and told her to fall in love with the children and make the best of her situation.

Jackie faced a tough challenge. Unfortunately, it's not so unusual. As a general rule, preschool children require approximately 35 square feet of floor space per child. Elementary children require approximately 25 square feet. How many churches have that much space? What can you do if the space you have is small, cluttered, poorly lit and unattractive? You'll be surprised at what a little creativity can accomplish!

♡ ♡ ♡ ♡ ♡ ♡ ♡ ♡ ♡ ♡ ♡ ♡ ♡

Getting Started

Begin by looking at individual elements of your teaching setting. Work with what you do have. Break your task into smaller challenges and attack them one by one. There are ways you can turn just about any little neck of the woods into a comfortable space kids can call their own.

9 Parts of a Captivating Classroom

- Doors That Dazzle
- Walls That Welcome
- Fabulous Floors
- Celestial Ceilings
- Centers That Captivate

- Fun Furniture
- Spectacular Scenery and Sets
- De-Lights!
- Wired for Sound

Doors That Dazzle

Every room has a door. Create excitement when children enter by **transforming your door into an intriguing entry that kids can't resist.** Shop at party stores to buy inexpensive "curtains" made from metallic ribbons, beads or streamers designed to hang in the doorway. Use large cardboard pieces to frame your door with murals that turn it into a cave, the mouth of an animals, a castle door, the doorway to a red barn—or anything else you can dream up! A church in Oklahoma constructed a small "caboose" doorway, complete with a train bell. The caboose was set within the existing doorway. Children love coming to their room, ringing the bell and entering through the "caboose."

Turn your door into a puppet stage! Cover a tension rod with a curtain and secure it inside the doorframe. Voilà! You can close the door while you install the puppet curtain. A puppet buddy standing by can knock. Picture the surprise on kids' faces when they open the door to see a puppet instead of a teacher!

To provide adequate safety and accountability, a door to a children's classroom needs to have a small window that allows a supervisor or ministry coordinator to observe the activity inside.

Walls That Welcome

Walls in most children's ministry facilities are white, gray or beige. Bo-o-o-ring! Take a look at the bright décor at kids' favorite places: toy stores, fast food chains and play centers. **Banish the beige!** Paint those walls in bright patterns and bold colors. If you have an artist in your church who is willing to paint a Bible story mural, so much the better.

If painting isn't an option, go the bulletin board and display route. Visit a teacher's store or a Christian supplier to check out all the incredible resources they have for creating bright bulletin boards. You'll find displays for an amazing number of themes and seasons. You can add color to walls simply and inexpensively by tacking up bright pieces of poster board where children can display their artwork, draw their names in big letters and write their prayer requests. Remember to place your wall displays at kids' eye level. If you share a room with other groups, set up a separate wall display for each program.

When you work with walls, remember that more isn't always better. Avoid the temptation to plaster every square inch with eye-popping color. For art to stand out and be noticed, leave some contrast in the background.

Children love to see their own artwork hung on walls. Seeing their own touch in the room gives kids an important sense of ownership. Ownership helps kids invest in what happens inside those walls. That means more motivation and cooperation on their part. So let kids make their mark!

If you're fortunate enough to have a window, celebrate the sunlight! Add a splash of color with curtains. Hang a sun catcher. Set a growing plant by the window and let the kids help you care for it.

Fabulous Floors

Have you ever noticed how much time kids spend on the floor? It's a natural environment for them. If you do all your teaching standing or sitting on a chair, you need to get down and join the fun. There's something wonderful about sitting cross-legged in a circle with your kids. Ladies, your teaching wardrobe needs to include long, full skirts. Gents, you have it made!

Keep floors clean and free of clutter, especially the nursery and preschool rooms.

Furniture in these rooms is not necessarily a plus. Little ones enjoy wide-open spaces! When you need to bring children into a group, use colorful carpet squares. Encourage kids to "plant" themselves on their squares and stay put until you put the squares away.

Large area rugs add color and dimension to your classroom. If you've been in a preschool lately you've probably noticed some of the great patterns that are available in kids' rugs these days. There are counting rugs, rugs with traffic patterns, flower rugs and patchwork rugs, just to name a few. A cozy rug with an exciting pattern that stirs kids' imaginations is well worth the investment.

You can use a rug to designate space for story time or a prayer circle. During a dramatic reenacting of a Bible story, a rug can become the palace in Egypt or the tabernacle where Samuel heard God or the Sea of Galilee. If you're part of a congregation that needs portability, go with a bright assortment of carpet squares instead.

Have you discovered the wonders of masking tape on your classroom floor? Masking tape can provide a great visual boundary to help kids know where to sit. You can also use colored electrical tape to mark off sections of your classroom for various centers and special activities. Make a giant tic-tac-toe board for elementary kids. Let the kids wear paper plates marked with Xs and Os. **Make the outline of a boat and invite everyone to be the disciples when you teach the story of Jesus calming the storm.** Let older children help you make a floor map of the journey to the Promised Land or Paul's missionary travels. Rope, clothesline and foil garlands can serve a similar function.

Celestial Ceilings

Look up! How is your ceiling constructed? Here's new space for teaching that you may not have considered before. Most ceilings in commercial buildings are "suspended ceilings" which consist of a metal grid with inlaid ceiling tiles. Local hardware stores carry plastic devices that hook right on the existing grillwork and allow you to hang all sorts of fun things: strands of curling ribbon, kids' artwork, teaching pictures and balloons to name a few.

Create booths and centers with bright shower curtains. Replace your boring ceiling with a false ceiling made by draping fabric over dowels that you hang at intervals across the room. Make a solid section of twisted crepe paper. Or take the leap and hang a colorful parachute!

A popular design, especially for older children, is an open ceiling effect. Remove the ceiling tiles and paint the rough ceiling a dark color. Black usually is best. Paint the heating and air conditioning tubes with bright primary colors. You may have to plead your case persuasively to the building committee, but kids will love it!

Centers That Captivate

Unless you have a tiny room, think seriously about setting aside space for learning centers. Centers allow children to move, explore and personally interact with the lesson. You'll capture a child's interest and imagination with something new and interesting in each center. And once you've created a center, it becomes a classroom helper you can count on week after week.

Create center spaces with masking tape, rope, curtains hung from the ceiling, tables and bookcases or other furniture. Label each center with foam core or poster board signs. Separate noisy centers from quiet centers. To use centers effectively, you'll need adequate adult supervision. How much supervision is required depends on the age of the children, number of children and the type of activity. Move children to the next center with a fun signal such as a bell, whistle or song.

Does your church pack up and move each week? Then do your centers in a suitcase! **The rolling variety is easy to get to and from your car. Stock each suitcase with art supplies, books, small audio equipment, or whatever captivates your kids.** You might even enlist a non-teaching volunteer to be your "center stocker" and take responsibility for creating and maintaining centers for your classroom.

Fun Furniture

Furniture can add to or distract from a creative classroom. Chairs should be low enough for children's feet to reach the floor. Use "chair smarts" when you set up each activity. When chairs are in a circle or around the perimeter of the room, everyone can see each other. A semi-circle arrangement helps kids focus on the teacher. If you set chairs up in rows, be sure to allow enough space between the rows so that kids can't put their feet on the backs of the chairs in front of them. Don't be afraid to lose chairs entirely. The image of children sitting quietly with their hands folded in their laps is not what you want! Kids need to be active and involved in every part of your lesson.

Learn to think of each piece of furniture as a story prop. Sometimes you need to turn the tables on kids—literally! Tables might best serve your lesson when they're upside-down! A boat…a house…a prison…what can your upside down table become? Or turn the table on its side to make the cave where Elijah heard God's whisper or to **create an instant puppet stage.** Drape it with a blanket to make a tent with David or Gideon the night before a battle. Table savvy is one of the best things you can have in your teacher's bag of tricks!

Plastic cubes are inexpensive, colorful and sturdy. Use them to make the walls of Jericho, to create a sheep pen or the stable where baby Jesus was born. Many churches share educational space between several programs. If keeping supplies and equipment separated is an issue, look into lockable storage cabinets.

Creative 10 Ideas for Learning Centers

- Story
- Nature
- Art
- Music
- Home living
- Blocks
- Books
- Puzzles
- Crafts
- Science

Think "safety first" when you place furniture in a children's classroom. Avoid rickety cast-offs. Make sure tables and chairs are sturdy enough to stand up to all the wiggly things kids like to do. Inspect each piece of furniture periodically for broken components or sharp edges. Cover sharp edges with rubber bumpers available at most hardware stores. Use shelves to keep items potentially dangerous to small children off the floor. Anchor to the wall any shelving that could tip over onto children.

Spectacular Scenery and Sets

Scenery and sets can transform any classroom into an on-site Bible experience. Sets can be extravagant or simple. Having permanent space for your children's ministry makes using sets easier, but if you share space or have to pack everything away each week, you can still create imaginative—but movable—sets. Transform large appliance boxes into portable sets that transport easily in and out of your room. Use the teenagers in your church as a resource both for creating and hauling the sets. Cut out shapes of Bible characters or objects in a story from foam core available from any craft store, and paint them.

Look around for ordinary objects that can add excitement to a Bible story, such as tents, blow-up boats, puppet stages and painted cardboard boxes. **If you've never pitched a tent in a classroom, try it this week.** You'll love the sheer delight on the faces of your kids as they see what you've done. (Have you ever taught in a pop-up camper set up in the parking lot? It makes a great mini-field trip for kids who need a break from the classroom!)

Paint a Backdrop

Paint a sheet with white latex paint and hang it on a wall. Use an overhead projector to display your pattern on the sheet. Trace the image onto the sheet and begin painting. Be sure to have cardboard or plastic under the sheet to prevent the paint from soaking through.

One children's minister painted a refrigerator box and called it the "time machine." With the addition of a fog machine and strobe light, the assistant teacher—dressed up as a Bible character—stepped out and told the Bible story while children sat spellbound. Another teacher took cardboard tubes from carpet rolls and built a log cabin using paper sacks as "chinking." **Be creative and let your imagination soar!** Our teaching should take children to the desert, an Egyptian palace, the Garden of Eden, the Sea of Galilee, or the temple where kids can experience the Bible story firsthand.

Scenery and props do not have to be complicated or permanent. They can be lightweight and portable. A blue blanket makes a very nice Sea of Galilee. Or a tent in the desert! Three sides of a cardboard box make a puppet stage that can be folded up and put away. Or a tabernacle. Or Mary and Martha's home. God gave children the gifts of imagination and creativity. It's part of the way they look at the world. "What could this be?" they ask. "What could I make?" Think like a child and have fun creating sets and scenery where the Bible can come alive.

De-Lights!

In the beginning God said, "Let there be light." Let there also be light in the children's classroom! Some children react very negatively to "fluorescent green" and the buzz of fluorescent lighting. Consider adding lighting with floor lamps or high wattage bulbs. No matter how many permanent lights you have in your room, you can add dramatic flair with special lighting effects for particular Bible stories. For instance:

☼ A bright spotlight helps illustrate the story of Jesus appearing to Saul on the road to Damascus.

☼ Don't forget the star that shown brightly over the place where baby Jesus was laid.

☼ Remember the light that beamed from the face of Moses after he received the Ten Commandments from God.

Sets that *Come Alive*

- Desert
- Ocean
- Garden
- Forest
- Temple
- Cave
- Wild West town
- Walking path
- Bible-time home
- Boat dock
- Cityscape
- Barnyard
- Jesus & the children
- Castle
- Train station
- Airport

☼ A flashlight makes a wonderful object lesson. The light won't come on without batteries. Jesus is our "battery" or power source that lives within us.

☼ Use a flashlight or lantern to illustrate Psalm 119:105, "Your word is a lamp to my feet and a light for my path."

☼ Use strobe lights to simulate lightning. If you don't have access to a strobe light, simply flash the room lights on and off. Let kids add thunder by pounding their feet. (Skip this last idea if there's another class below you!)

☼ Black lights are common in puppetry and provide an effect that makes children squeal with delight. Black light is ultraviolet light. Certain colors and paints will fluoresce under black light. Create visuals, signs and puppet props with florescent paint and illuminate them with ultraviolet light. Most major department or lighting stores carry inexpensive black light fixtures.

☼ Decorate your room, bulletin board border or doorway with multi-colored flashing Christmas tree lights.

☼ Make a campfire with flashlights and rolled-up newspapers. Sit around the fire and share faith stories.

Now you're thinking! You'll have the COOLEST, most child-friendly class in your church.

Some Bible stories require darkness. When God created the world, darkness covered the face of the earth. In Exodus God sent darkness throughout Egypt for the ninth plague. Perhaps it was dark in the lions' den for Daniel. When Jesus was crucified, everything became dark, even during daytime. Older kids may be comfortable in a dark environment with black plastic taped over the window. Or save yourself some work and travel to the furnace room for moments of darkness. Let kids know you have a flashlight close by. With preschoolers, however, darkness can be a fearful thing. Drape a table and crawl under it rather than darkening the whole room. Create a sense of coziness with a small flashlight. And stay in the darker environment for just a short period of time.

Small, squeezable key-chain flashlights create the warm glow of candlelight without the risk. They're a wonderful small gift that kids will cherish. Imagine Gideon's soldiers with mini-flashlights in hand conquering the bewildered enemy. What a treat! An unforgettable Bible story is more than enough reason to go for the glow.

Wired for Sound

In effective children's ministry classrooms, great sounds abound! And we're not talking about sound systems that cost hundreds of dollars. Most portable stereos make great classroom sound systems. And many come in kid-friendly colors and formats. There's no greater honor for a child than to be your designated "sound technician" of the day!

Whatever atmosphere you're trying to create, sound sets the stage! Do you want kids to experience a friendly welcome? **Play lively music that invites interaction.** Do you want kids to calm down for a quiet, reflective activity? Soft praise music does the trick. Do you want to energize kids for games? Pump up the volume! There is such a wealth of Christian music available. If your church doesn't have an appropriate library of CDs, get together with other teachers and start one. Add some inexpensive sound effects CDs to give your Bible stories realism and drama.

Use a cassette tape to record the voice of a Bible character actor. And don't forget, kids love to hear themselves. Keep a cassette recorder in a learning center so kids can record their own radio reports, interviews and first-person accounts.

One of the most effective and lasting uses of music is in Bible memory. Unfortunately, many children's programs have strayed from this invaluable tool. Make Scripture stick in your kids' minds by choosing material that offers Bible memory music. You'll be amazed how many Bible verses make it into kids' memories even when they're just played as background music.

Even if you are not musically gifted, you can effectively use music in your classroom. Set notes dancing in your kids' minds every time you teach. The message behind the notes will dance right into their hearts and minds

♡ ♡ ♡ ♡ ♡ ♡ ♡ ♡ ♡ ♡ ♡ ♡

Classrooms on the Move

A significant number of churches meet in rented or temporary facilities such as schools, convention centers, office buildings, hotels, theaters and community centers. When children's ministry programs meet in these temporary facilities, it's a special challenge to design creative learning environments. But it can be done, and it can be fun!

If your classroom moves each week, you need to be prepared, organized and on top of things so you can focus your attention on kids instead of on getting your teaching tools together. Rolling suitcases and storage tubs will be your friends!

Perhaps there's a storage closet in the rented facility that's available to you. That makes life easier! Engage older kids to be your set-up crew and haul designated containers from the storage area to your classroom. If you need to take everything home each week, allow yourself 10 or 15 extra minutes on each end of your ministry time. Kids consider it an honor to

Split-Track—a Must!

If you're buying a new portable stereo to use in children's ministry, choose one that plays "split tracks." Split-track format is a recording method that allows you to hear the instruments only by turning the balance to the left. To hear the voices only, turn the balance to the right. An equal balance plays both instruments and voices. Select a system that plays both CDs and cassettes. CDs allow random access selection of each song recorded on the disk. This is very helpful in teaching and leading children in music.

help "teacher" bring things in from the car. They'll learn to anticipate the appearance of their favorite centers and props.

Glance through this list of portable classroom tactics. See what sparks an idea that will work for you.

☼ Instead of one long rod to hang a curtain, use PVC pipes that come apart to store.

☼ Choose carpet squares over area rugs.

☼ Collect colorful plastic tablecloths that fold easily and quickly brighten a classroom.

☼ Create portable bulletin boards out of colored 2′ x 3′ foam core from an office supply or craft store.

☼ If you have a blank wall, be on the lookout for transparencies of Bible story art.

☼ Collect several smaller plastic containers of a uniform stacking size that fit in the larger tub. Use these for keeping craft items and teaching supplies sorted.

The Safety Test

CLASSROOM SAFETY CONSIDERATIONS

- ○ Cleanliness
- ○ Pleasant odor
- ○ Covered electrical outlets
- ○ Anchored shelves
- ○ Age-appropriate furniture
- ○ Sharp edges covered
- ○ Accessible first aid kit
- ○ Accessible fire extinguisher
- ○ Posted evacuation plan
- ○ Check-in/check-out procedure
- ○ Team teaching approach
- ○ Room sign designation
- ○ Nursery & preschool on ground floor
- ○ Door with a window

☼ Make a colorful portable backdrop on a sheet.

☼ Help children create individual "portfolios" in a colorful folder. Over a period of several weeks, kids can create a keepsake that chronicles spiritual learning. Portfolios can also be colorful, private learning spaces and a sense of ownership in an otherwise impersonal room. In between teaching sessions, the portfolios can be stacked and stored.

Church members in a temporary space are usually good sports about volunteering to help with set-up and tear-down. Don't be the Lone Ranger in your efforts to make a fun, fascinating classroom. Enlist a committed group of people to come to your aid each week so that you can focus your energy on your kids.

Alternative Classrooms

Five-year-old Molly waved at her dad with one hand while she held on to a long rope with the rest of the kindergarten class. "We're on a field trip!" she excitedly told her dad, who was surprised to see her in the hall during the middle of Sunday school. Molly's teacher was taking the class on a trip to the temple in Jerusalem—the church's worship center.

A great children's ministry leader once said that creative teachers develop new ways to teach old truths without worrying about failures or limitations. If facilities become a major limitation, think creatively. Within and around the church you'll find many spaces just waiting to be used as alternative classrooms. Moving kids to another location periodically will add a new dimension to your teaching. Think about the building that you teach in. What interesting places could you explore with your class in upcoming weeks?

☑ Auditorium	☑ Playground	☑ Tree
☑ Hallway	☑ Parking lot	☑ Nursery
☑ Kitchen	☑ Maintenance room	☑ Choir room
☑ Pastor's study	☑ Basement	☑ Baptistry
☑ Gymnasium	☑ Library	☑ Courtyard
☑ Soundroom	☑ Church bus	

Pause Point

Interesting places in my church building:

1.

2.

3.

A really enterprising teacher might venture beyond the building and grounds. This can be a great energizer for both the teacher and the students. A real-life setting can bring a Bible story to life in a way that doesn't happen in a classroom. Field trips

Bulletin Boards on the Move

You can make a portable bulletin board or teaching boards from colored foam core. Standard foam core is white, but many colors are available. Add a bulletin board border to the foam core and then laminate the entire board. Then use duct tape to attach the board to a freestanding, collapsible stand that sets on a table. You can put two foam core pieces together for a larger display area.

require permission slips and extra helpers, but they're worth the extra effort.

Any environment that causes a child to personally experience a Bible story more fully can become a children's ministry classroom. When Jesus taught his followers the many lessons found in the Gospels, he didn't have a classroom with four walls. **The whole world became his classroom.** Jesus taught people in a field, by a well, on a donkey, from a boat, on a mountain, on the beach, in a home, and even on a cross. Consider "on-site" classrooms the next time you're teaching one of these Bible lessons:

- Pond or lake (Jesus walked on the water)
- Spring (living water)
- Bridge (Christ is our bridge to heaven)
- House (Jesus eats with sinners)
- Cemetery (resurrection)
- Nursing home (serving)
- Funeral home (death)
- Shopping mall (materialism)
- Farm (sower and the seeds)
- Zoo (creation or the story of Noah)
- Military base (Christian basic training)
- Garden (Garden of Eden)
- Running track (pressing on toward the prize)
- School (study to show yourself approved)
- Baseball field (Christian growth)
- Mountaintop (Jesus is tempted)
- Orchard (bearing fruit or vine and branches)
- Lighthouse (let your light shine)
- Landfill (don't accumulate treasures on earth)
- Boat (Jesus calms the storm)
- Fishing dock (Jonah flees to Tarshish)

- Construction site (wise and foolish builders)
- Sewage treatment plant (God wants us to live pure lives)
- Printing company (we should spread the Good News)
- Laundromat (Jesus cleanses us from all sin)
- Water well (the woman at the well)
- Walking path (Good Samaritan)

Jesus taught people IN A FIELD, by a well, on a donkey, from a boat, on a mountain, on the beach, in a home, and even on a CROSS.

Make the Most of Wherever You Are

Doorways, walls, floors, ceilings, centers, furniture, sets, lighting and sound. Portable classrooms. Alternative classrooms. **Is there such a thing as a "typical" children's ministry classroom?** Every setting has its advantages and challenges. Where does that leave Jackie in her seven-by-ten storage room? Or the teacher in the furnace room? Or the one in borrowed classroom space where the children are asked not to touch anything? Or the class that has to finish early so the choir can come in and practice?

Maybe you don't have wall space, but you do have a floor. Maybe you don't have an elaborate set, but you do have a blanket and a stack of towels. Maybe you can't hang anything on the wall, but you can turn the table on its side. And you might just turn your children's ministry upside down in the process! **Remember, you have an ally in your kids' imaginations.** And you'll gain their appreciation with every creative turn you take in making a welcoming, kid-friendly space for them to learn God's Word.

Pause Point

What "alternative classrooms" can you drive to in less than 10 minutes from your church? Ask a group of parents to help you transport children, and plan an outing that fits within your teaching time frame.

Bible story:

Lesson point:

Where:

When:

Arrangements:

   •Permissions:

   •Parent helpers:

   •Transportation:

Chapter 7

Have You lost your Senses?

Mrs. Briggs teaches second grade Sunday school at Wilson Community Church. Every Sunday children love to come to Mrs. Briggs's class.

Last Sunday was no exception. The lesson featured the Bible story of Jesus calming the storm. The class began when Mrs. Briggs asked if anyone ever felt afraid. Of course all the children raised their hands.

"What causes you to be afraid?" asked Mrs. Briggs. Mean people, storms, spiders, snakes, doctors and the dark.

"If you thought you might drown, would you be afraid?" asked Mrs. Briggs. Eyes wide, heads bobbing, the kids said yes.

"Would you like to hear about some grown-ups who were so afraid one day that they cried out to Jesus while he was sleeping?"

For the next 40 minutes, Mrs. Briggs captivated the children. They built an imaginary boat out of chairs and rope. They took turns acting out the Bible story. Mrs. Briggs played a sound effects tape to simulate a storm while the children made rain and thunder by snapping their fingers, patting their legs and stomping their feet. She even prepared the room with "a sea breeze" air freshener and gently sprayed each child with a mist of water when the storm arose in the story.

Tommy played the role of Jesus. At Mrs. Briggs's signal, he stood in the back of the boat and yelled, **"Peace, be still!"** Suddenly everything became calm. The winds stopped blowing, the waves stopped rolling, and the rain stopped falling. Everyone shouted, "even the winds and the waves obey him." Mrs. Briggs followed the story with an appropriate song and a discussion about peace and how Jesus can help us even when we are afraid.

Second graders at Wilson Community Church wouldn't miss Sunday school for the world. They also believe that Mrs. Briggs is the best teacher in the whole wide world. The reason? Mrs. Briggs understands children and the way they enjoy learning. She also understands one of the most basic techniques for effective teaching: she uses teaching methods that incorporate all five senses.

Hotlines to the Brain

Multisensory learning combines multiple senses in a single learning task. Viewing a video of Jesus calming the storm combines auditory and visual elements. Acting out the story through drama while being sprayed with a mist of water involves the senses of touch and hearing. Both are examples of multisensory learning.

Multisensory learning is not new. It's been around for thousands of years! **Jesus himself taught people using multisensory techniques.** Jesus called attention to the birds and urged his followers to consider how the birds do not sow, reap or have a storeroom. "God feeds them," he said. "See how the lilies of the field grow. They do not labor or spin. Yet I tell you, not even Solomon in all his splendor was dressed like one of these" (Matthew 6:26–29). Jesus sat down at a well with a woman from Samaria and told her that he could give living water to satisfy her deep thirst. Jesus touched the eyes of the blind and they received their sight. He washed the disciples' feet as he shared a lesson about serving others.

Senses are a direct "hotline" to the brain. Sensory information bombards us every moment of the day. Even when we are least aware of it, our senses constantly send thousands of messages to the brain. Walking down the hall sends sensory data up through your feet. A breeze fluttering against your skin sends a message to your brain. Everything you see, hear, smell or touch sends information to your brain. Computers, home theaters, electronic games and a host of other technological gadgets immerse the consumer in a modern multisensory experience.

Research indicates that each sense stores the information it receives in a different place in the brain. When we use a teaching strategy that involves more than one sense, we increase the number of connections being made in the brain—and the likelihood that the children will be able to recall that information later.

We tend to remember 10% of what we read, 20% of what we hear and 30% of what we see. Few Sunday school teachers would consider their teaching successful if their students retained 30% or less of the Bible lesson. When hearing and seeing are combined, however, the retention level increases to 50%. Children remember 70% of what they say and 90% of what they say and do. **By incorporating verbal, visual, tactile, and kinesthetic (body movement) activities in our teaching, we really can teach so that children learn—and remember!**

Not all students learn in the same way. Most very young children are tactile kinesthetic learners. They need to handle things and move around. As they grow they develop other learning preferences: hearing and talking, seeing and writing, touching and hands-on manipulation, full body movement.

> ✯Approximately 20% of people are auditory learners; they learn best by hearing.
>
> ✯20% are visual; they learn best by seeing.
>
> ✯40% are tactile/kinesthetic; they need to touch, feel, and move around. That's a big percentage. Are kids doing art, science and craft projects in your classroom? Are they acting out stories? Playing meaningful games?
>
> ✯Here's something that won't surprise you if you're an observer of people: a far greater percentage of males are tactile/kinesthetic learners than females.
>
> ✯Some people don't have a strong learning preference but do well with any teaching method.

Children also differ in how they respond to environmental conditions such as sound, lights, temperature and time of day. Some learn best with brightly-lit conditions while others prefer soft lighting. Some prefer a quiet atmosphere while others enjoy noise. Some students learn best in a warm and cozy environment and others do better when the temperature is cool. Some prefer learning during early hours while others are at their peak in late afternoon or evening.

Limiting teaching strategies to your own preferences for learning means you won't reach all students in a way that makes it possible for them to learn. Broaden your array of teaching methods and renew enthusiasm for teaching in the process. You'll also help kids become more successful at learning in your classroom.

Does It Really Matter?

So what's all the fuss about learning styles and multisensory learning? Consider these truths:

☼: Our five senses are the primary way information goes to the brain. Use as many of the five senses as you can to get the most out of a teaching activity.

☼: When a learning activity appeals to two or more senses, more learning happens.

☼: When you use multiple senses, you reduce boredom. When you reduce boredom, you reduce behavior problems.

☼: Smelling and tasting activities can be the most effective in learning, but they are the least used.

☼: Learning activities that allow children to say or do something result in greatest ability to recall and demonstrate what they've learned.

☼: Effective teaching values the differences among children. God created each child to be unique. Plan varied teaching activities to meet varied needs. Change the learning environment from time to time.

Avoid the temptation to use only methods that appeal to YOUR OWN individual learning styles.

Sometimes when we think kids are not paying attention, what we really mean is, "Filter out all that other sensory data and focus on the sensory data I'm giving you with my voice." That's an adult perspective. Kids do more than one thing at a time all the time. And they learn a lot along the way. Make the most of this in your classroom.

Making a sensory-rich classroom doesn't have to be complicated. When you're planning an activity, close your eyes for a moment and imagine what the kids are doing. Are they moving? Are they holding anything? Are they listening for something special? Are they watching something intriguing? When you think they should be sitting and listening to the Bible story, Jake will be rolling on his back, and Lizzy will be reading what's on the bulletin board behind you. How can you add kinesthetic and visual elements to your storytelling and capture both Jake and Lizzy?

No one teacher can remember a library of multisensory learning activities. That's why every teacher needs several good resource books and a Bible curriculum that incorporates loads of multisensory learning activities.

ℒearning by Hearing

Hearing is perhaps the most used teaching method—all the way up through boring college lectures. Traditionally, having children listen is basic to the storytelling that is at the heart of Bible learning. But learning by hearing doesn't mean nothing else can be going on. You can enrich a story with simple things: recorded music, sound effects, videos, singing, dramatic readings, puppets, quiz games, musical instruments. Kids who are auditory learners often do well in cooperative projects where talking about what they're learning is part of the task.

Making Sense of It All

For most kids, figuring out what sensory information is important to pay attention to is a process that involves maturity. The preschool child is easily distracted from your voice by the paper wad that whizzes by. An older child might notice the paper wad but remain focused on what you're saying. Some adults get to the point where they don't even notice the paper wad!

Some unusual kids have a true sensory integration disorder. They really do have trouble sorting out what sensory information is important to pay attention to. For instance, they may not be able to single out your voice as important against background noise. Or the hardness of the chair beneath them will seem just as important as the paper on the table before them. In that case overstimulation of the senses can interfere with learning. If you suspect you have a child like this in your class, look for a role that gives that child less sensory stimulation than the rest of the class gets.

Learning by Seeing

Visual learners benefit from looking at something. Words or pictures are the most common visual focal points in traditional learning environments. Hearing is often combined with seeing, such as when teachers use puppets, pictures, flannel figures or felt, videos or overhead transparencies. But you can give kids even more intriguing things to watch:

- Mime
- Drama
- Object lessons
- A demonstration
- A story where the teacher creates a visual while telling the story

You can also involve kids in creating visual elements to use in the class:

- Banners
- Bulletin boards
- Models, exhibits, displays
- Story backgrounds

Use technology to enhance a visual experience, such as computers or lighting effects.

Learning by Touching

Some kids need to be moving or touching something in order to learn best. There's a reason why Josh likes to fidget with a toy car during the children's ministry program, or why Nellie likes to hug her teddy bear while she listens to the story.

Simple objects can bring a Bible story TO LIFE when children get to touch them.

Why not put something related to the story in Josh's hands? Or give Nellie something from the story to hold and interact with? Here's a list to get your collection started:

Seashells	Creation or any of the stories involving seas or oceans
Water	Creation, crossing the Red Sea, the Flood, baptism of Jesus
Rocks	Stoning of Stephen, rocks turned to bread in the temptation of Jesus, and five smooth stones in the story of David and Goliath
Baby	Birth of Jesus or any other child
Plants	Creation or Moses among the riverbank reeds
Sand	Wise and foolish builders
Coins	30 pieces of silver paid to Judas for betraying Jesus
Bread	Jesus is the Bread of Life
Corn	Pig feed that the prodigal son wanted to eat
Shepherd's staff	David, the shepherd king, Jesus is our Good Shepherd
Bandages	The good Samaritan helped the traveler
Slingshot	Used by David to defeat Goliath
Thorns	Placed on Jesus' head during crucifixion
Sword	Used by Peter to cut off Roman soldier's ear
Chains	Paul and Silas bound in prison
Seeds	Parable of sower and the seed
Hair	Samson and Delilah
Foot washing	Jesus washes his disciples' feet
Clay	God is the potter; we are clay
Olive oil	David is anointed as king; anointing the sick with oil
Hugs	Jesus loves children
Heater	Three Hebrew young men thrown into the fiery furnace
Palm branches	Jesus' triumphal entry into Jerusalem
Fruit	First sin by Adam and Eve
Sandpaper	God is able to smooth our rough edges
Roofing tar	Noah coated the ark with pitch
Armor	The armor of God and David and Goliath
Engraving	The 10 Commandments engraved on tablets of stone
Pearls	In all things God works things together for our good

Learning by Tasting

"Snack time" is a given in many children's ministry programs. But you can use food for learning, not just for filling time or rumbly tummies. Use food that represents something concrete in the story. Use it to build a miniature version of something in the story. Use it as art. **Munching time is a good time to talk about story review or application.** Here are a few ideas to get you started.

Pudding in a jar: Creation

We can't create from nothing like God can. But we can make pudding from milk and a mix if we carefully follow instructions. Place 2 1/2 tablespoons of instant pudding and 1/4 cup milk in each jar. Tightly screw on lids. Have the class shake their jars as they count to 20 three times. Let each jar set for about five minutes. Watch as children enjoy their smooth creations.

Animal cookies and sunflower seeds: Creation

Discuss all the kinds of animals and birds that God created and the different kinds of seed birds eat.

People-shaped cookies or bread cutouts: God creates the first people

Talk about how God created man and woman and how special we are as part of his creation.

Marshmallows: Samson

Explain that Samson was a very strong man. Give each child a toothpick and two marshmallows. Demonstrate how to make weight-lifting barbells by pushing one marshmallow onto each end of the toothpick.

Various fruit: Creation and the first sin

Review the tree of the knowledge of good and evil, and how Eve sinned when she ate the fruit God told her not to.

Gummy worms, gummy fish or goldfish crackers: **Jonah**

Enhance the story about Jonah and how a big fish swallowed him with food. The Bible explains that it was a big fish. Fish do not usually swallow people for food. In fact, when we go fishing, we use worms for bait, not people!

Instant grape drink mix: **The first miracle**

Show the children how to make grape drink mix by using the mix, sugar, and water. Tell the children how Jesus changed water into wine without using any other ingredient. Jesus could do miracles. Then allow the children to enjoy the refreshing drink.

Red gelatin: **Moses and the Red Sea**

Show the children how the Red Sea parted by using red gelatin in a flat dish. Remove a middle section of gelatin until you have a "walkway" from end to end. (Save this for the children to eat.) Cover the gelatin with plastic wrap and let the children walk their fingers down the middle the way the Israelites walked through the Red Sea.

Leavened and unleavened bread and grapes: **The Last Supper**

Before the children arrive, set up your classroom tables banquet-style with nice dishes, silverware, napkins and cups or goblets for a feast. Tell the children the story of the Last Supper. Allow the children to taste the difference between leavened and unleavened bread, and explain why it was served. Share the meaning of the wine—made from grapes—which represented the blood of Jesus. Afterward serve the remaining bread with butter and jelly.

Angel-shaped cookies or bread cutouts: **Birth of Jesus**

Find an angel-shaped cookie cutter and make cookies for (or with) the children. Have the children decorate them. Remind the children that Gabriel was the angel that told Mary she was going to have a special baby named Jesus.

Shredded wheat cereal: **Birth of Jesus**

Use shredded wheat cereal to represent the hay that surrounded baby Jesus in the manger. Then pretend your children are a flock of sheep and let them gobble down the hay.

Grilled cheese sandwiches or cheese and crackers: **David and Goliath**

Share the story of how David's father had sent him to the army camp where his brothers were fighting Goliath. He was taking bread and cheese to his brothers.

Tuna fish sandwiches: **The boy who shared his lunch**

Tell the children how a little boy shared his small lunch of fish and bread and how Jesus used it to feed over 5,000 men plus women and children. Then pretend you are listening to Jesus as the disciples serve you bread and fish.

Star-shaped cookies with bright sprinkles: **The wisemen visit Jesus**

Use either store-bought cookies that already have green or red sprinkles or allow the children to put sprinkles on their own cookies. Tell the children about the star that led the wisemen to Jesus and how extra big and bright it was.

Corn on the cob: **The prodigal son**

Serve corn on the cob with butter and salt and show the children what a corncob looks like after they finish eating. The son who left home eventually had to work at a pig farm in order to survive. He wished he could eat what the pigs ate. Many times pigs ate cornhusks or cobs.

Mixed colored candy: **Joseph and the coat of many colors**

Show the children the different pretty-colored candies. Let them represent the colors in Joseph's coat. Following the story, everyone gets to munch on the sweet candy.

Blue gelatin:
The tempest stilled/Jesus walks on water

Serve blue gelatin to the children while sharing the story of Jesus calming the storm or Jesus walking on the water to the disciples.

Gumdrops and pretzels: Various stories

Allow the children to use gumdrops and pretzel sticks to build objects in a story: prisons, palaces, boats, people, temples, crosses and other objects.

Pigs in a blanket: Elijah's prayer power

Serve the children "pigs in a blanket" (mini-hot dogs rolled in biscuit dough and baked) while telling the story of how God sent ravens with meat and bread to feed Elijah during a drought.

Pancakes:
Elijah and the widow of Zarephath:

Tell the children the story of Elijah and the widow of Zarephath and how God multiplied the two food items the widow had: flour and oil. Use the flour and oil along with other ingredients to make pancakes on an electric griddle before their very eyes. Then serve pancakes to everyone.

Egg salad sandwiches:
Jesus lives for us

Take a raw egg and remove the yoke and white by poking small holes at the ends of the egg and blowing from one end out the other. Show the children another egg and crack it in front of them to show what is in an egg. This egg will represent tombs of people who have died. Then take the empty egg and crack it in front of the children and show them that Jesus' tomb was unlike others, it was empty! Then share egg salad sandwiches with the children.

Applesauce: Baby Moses or Samuel

When telling any story that involves babies, serve the children applesauce—an appropriate food for babies to eat.

Kiwi fruit: **Jacob and Esau**

When telling the story of Jacob and Esau, use kiwi with its "hairy" texture to represent Esau. Cut the fruit in cross sections. Place several pieces on a paper plate along with pretzel sticks to make Esau. Cross sections of bananas with its smooth texture can represent Jacob. Then let the children nibble the brothers.

Beef jerky: **Daniel in the lions' den**

Let children munch on beef jerky as you tell the story of Daniel and the lion's den. The main food for lions is meat. Since lions really like meat, it was a miracle of God that they didn't eat Daniel.

Honey: **Various stories**

Serve honey to the children when telling children how John the Baptist ate honey. The promised land was a land filled with "milk and honey." Psalm 119:103 compares God's Word to sweet honey.

Sour candy: **Bitter water at Marah**

After the Israelites traveled for three days in the desert, they came to Marah where the water was bitter. Allow the children to taste the sour candy and compare the bitterness of the candy to the bitterness of Marah's water.

♡ ♡ ♡ ♡ ♡ ♡ ♡ ♡ ♡ ♡

Learning by Smelling

Do you remember what your grandmother's house smelled like when you were little and the gas heater in the hall came on? Or your father's aftershave when he tucked you into bed with a kiss? Or the scent of the first flowers anyone ever gave you? Smell is a powerful sense, digging up memories we might have thought were beyond reach. An infant first bonds with its mother though the sense of smell. Imagine how powerful smell can be in creating memory hooks for kids learning Bible stories. It's not as hard as you might think to bring the sense of smell into your lesson. Here are some easy ideas.

Fresh flowers: **Jesus' betrayal**

Bring in fresh flowers for the children to smell and tell how Jesus prayed in the Garden of Gethsemane before he was betrayed and taken away. Fresh flowers can also be used to describe the Garden of Eden.

Vinegar: **Jesus died for us**

Allow the children to smell vinegar as you tell them how the soldiers tried to get Jesus to drink vinegar to quench his thirst.

Hay: **Jesus' Birth or Noah's ark**

Bring hay into the class for the children to sit on and smell. Jesus' bed was made of hay. Noah must have had bales of hay for the animals.

Fragrant candles: **The magi visit Jesus**

Before the children arrive, light fragrant candles. Use the fragrance to remind the children of the gift of incense the magi brought to baby Jesus.

Perfumes: **A woman shows her love for Jesus**

Bring several bottles of perfume to class for the children to smell. Have a contest on the best-smelling perfume. Tell the children how a woman washed Jesus' feet with a very expensive perfume.

Tuna fish: **Jonah**

Open a can of tuna before class so that the smell will permeate the room. Discuss with the children how the inside of a fish must have smelled.

Various smells: **Blind Bartimaeus**

Bring several items with strong odors to class and have the children close their eyes and try to guess what the items are. (Vanilla, vinegar, lemon and hand lotion work well.) Blind people like Bartimaeus rely more on the sense of smell than we do.

Baby powder: **Baby Moses or Samuel**

Have children apply a small amount of baby powder to their hands. Talk about the special smell that babies have. Lead into a story about a special baby.

"Sea breeze" air freshener: **Jesus calms the storm**

Spray the room with the air freshener scented like the ocean to create a memorable oceanic experience.

Matches or charred wood: **The fiery furnace, burning bush, and tongues**

Light a match in front of the children and let them smell the air. You can also place a piece of charred wood in the room to create a similar odor. Discuss what a fire smells like as you tell the story of the fiery furnace or burning bush.

Various fruits, vegetables and flowers: **Creation**

Bring in various fruits, vegetables and flowers and keep them covered or disguised. Have the children close their eyes and smell the different items and try to guess what the object is. Discuss the unique plants and fragrances that God created.

Lotions: **Queen Esther**

Let children smell different lotions as small amounts are applied to each of them. Tell the story of Esther and how she was chosen as the new queen of Persia. Before she was chosen, several young women who competed for queen received beauty treatments.

Medicines and vitamins: **The good Samaritan**

Let children sniff various medicines (alcohol, ointments, vitamins). Tell the children how the Good Samaritan helped the hurt man and doctored his wounds.

Leavened and unleavened bread, grape juice or wine: **The Last Supper**

Let the children smell the bread, juice or wine, the sacred elements of communion.

Cooking odors:
Mary and Martha or Jacob and Esau

As you tell the story of Mary and Martha entertaining Jesus in their home or Jacob stealing Esau's birthright, cook something yummy like soup to create a home living atmosphere.

Fresh fruit: Fruit of the Spirit

Fruit such as pineapples and oranges can provide pungent odors as you teach the children about the fruit of the Spirit.

Dead fish: Plague, river turned to blood

Purchase some fish at a fish market. Allow the odor to fill the classroom as you tell the children about the first plague God sent upon the Egyptians (the rivers turning to blood). The Bible says that the fish died and the terrible odor was everywhere.

Scented lamp oil: Parable of the 10 maidens

Bring a small container of lamp oil. As you tell the children the story of the ten maidens, light the wick and allow the children to smell the odor.

Burned food: Burned offering

Jewish laws and customs included offering burnt sacrifices. Set a plate of burned hamburgers, hot dogs or chicken out so everyone can see and smell.

Pine or ammonia cleanser: Cleansed from sin

Jesus wants to cleanse our lives from sin. Discuss how dirty our houses become and how often we need to clean them. Let the children smell the cleansers and talk about the clean smell.

Moldy bread: Manna gathered on the Sabbath

Allow a loaf of bread to mold and become very smelly. Tell the children how manna collected on the Sabbath would become bad and stink. Let the children see and smell the moldy bread.

Garbage: Sin

Bring a small, double-wrapped bag of smelly garbage to the classroom or set it outdoors. Tell the children that sin is a lot like garbage. It really stinks and should be removed. Remove the garbage and tell the children how God can forgive us if we ask him.

Paint: Pharisees whitewashed tombs

Jesus called the Pharisees "whitewashed tombs." They looked good on the outside but inside they were dead and full of sin. Paint an old rotten board to illustrate and allow the odor to fill the room.

As you scanned through these ideas, you probably thought, "I could do that." And you can! If you look through your cupboards and cabinets, you'd probably find pudding and cleanser and fragrances and bread and matches. You'll find a lot of other things not listed here that would make great sensory jumping-off points in a lesson or that can become part of the story environment. **Turn your classroom into a rich sensory learning environment!** You'll have lessons that kids will remember. And they'll remember you because of your extra efforts to make learning fun for them!

8 Speed-bumps, Roadblocks and Dried-out Markers

She walked into her meticulously decorated classroom, well prepared for the upcoming lesson.

Her students stood and said in chorus, "Good morning."

"Good morning, everyone," she replied. "You may be seated." As a well-trained choir, they sat in one movement. She graciously smiled. "Please open your Bibles to the Gospel of John."

The lesson flowed smoothly. Every child eagerly participated, each knowing every answer to every question. They supported and encouraged one another. They were polite, well mannered and a joy to teach. Never once during the hour did a disruption occur, a crayon break, or a Bible page tear. It was perfect.

Then she woke up.

Stealing a glance at the clock as she catapulted into the bathroom, she saw she was already 10 minutes behind schedule. As she slid into the car, she remembered that car windows should remain up during rainstorms—the backside of her already wrinkled skirt was now also soaked. She hit every single red light between her apartment and the church. The parking lot was full, so she had to park in the grass. As she raced across the field, muddy water squished through her toes, turning her white sandals into a strange shade of taupe.

The children's ministry director handed off lesson materials like a baton as she shot past him. She entered the room breathlessly. The ruckus she had heard upon entering the church building suddenly silenced. Twelve seven-year-old faces turned toward her, looked through her as if she were invisible, then turned back. The ruckus resumed.

The lesson flowed like molasses in a creek bed. Every child eagerly participated—just not in the manner she had hoped. The children teased and laughed with one another. One rocked in his chair the entire lesson, falling backward four times. A second child blew his very stuffy nose—without a tissue. Another stubbed her toe and cried for 12 minutes. Still another wanted to sing "100 Bottles of Beer on the Wall." (When she suggested that song wasn't quite appropriate, he said they could change it to "root beer." He was sure Jesus liked to drink root beer.) The rainstorm from the night before began again. (Guess who still hadn't rolled up the car window?) Lightning cracked and the lights flickered off for a moment.

Later she learned that **just as the pastor had said, "and the cries of the demons could be heard," the screams of her twelve 7 year olds reverberated throughout the sanctuary.**

And when the children's parents came to collect them, she gave each one a hug and spoke words of affirmation. By the time she finished sharing a hug with each of the 12, she had a red handprint on her left shoulder, a smear of grape jelly at her waist, Billy's take-home paper stuck firmly to the bottom of one of her muddy shoes and some purple glitter sparkled in her hair.

She sat down on a chair that supported only half of what she needed supported, and sighed. That's when Billy sauntered back in and nonchalantly peeled his take-home paper off the sole of her shoe. "I like this story," he said. "I want to show my mom."

It was then she realized that although she hadn't prepared as she should have, although almost every disruption imaginable occurred, although her classroom management skills left much to be desired that morning and the kids had been well into the wild side, she had touched the life of at least one child. It hadn't been perfect, but they'd made it.

If this story rang all-too-familiar with you, you're most likely a veteran of the wonderful world of teaching. We've all been there at one time or another—which is why the children's ministry director didn't mention anything about running late. He knew first-hand what kind of day she was having.

Let's face it. We all have days when our clothes are wrinkled, our shoes muddied, our brains fuzzy, our schedules shot and our attitudes not quite so great. Does that mean that God cannot or will not use us? Absolutely not.

Look at the men and women in the Bible God used for marvelous and life-changing moments. He took their weaknesses and moments of complete uselessness and turned them upside-down. You may as well give up on your excuses right now!

- Moses stuttered.
- Abraham was too old.
- Ruth didn't belong.
- Obadiah was too obscure.
- Naomi was a widow.
- Solomon was too rich.
- Jeremiah was depressed.
- Samson had long hair.
- John Mark was rejected by Paul.
- Matthew was a disliked publican.
- Thomas doubted.
- Peter was afraid of death.
- John the Baptist was a wild man.

- David was too young.
- Hosea's wife was a prostitute.
- Amos's only training was in fig-tree pruning.
- Job was going through way too much.
- Rahab had a reputation.
- Jonah ran from God.
- Elijah was burned-out.
- David's armor didn't fit.
- Moses was a murderer. So was Paul.
- Timothy had ulcers.
- Mary was lazy.
- Martha was a worrywart.
- And Lazarus was dead.

God will use us in spite of who we are. And in the process he'll change us into who he created us to be.

Teaching will always have its moments of complete mayhem. If you're just entering this exciting world, take it as fact that you'll hit speedbumps along the way. And if you've been in children's ministry for a long time, you already know that the roadblocks never completely disappear. This mayhem may spring from a multitude of causes—anything from your own daftness when you leave the entire lesson book at home, to Freddy losing his breakfast, to the fire drill that occurs right in the middle of Tymora's prayer for salvation. Expect the unexpected. Be prepared for times of confusion and go with the flow.

𝒜 FUNtastic First Day

Everyone has heard the advice "Be tough at first. Then you can ease up when they know who is boss." Phooey. Don't believe them. They're from the "old school" of thought, and we're now in the twenty-first century. Kids are smart. They can see through such tactics like Superman sees through walls. Besides, what exactly are you teaching them through that type of behavior? That you earn respect through being a bully?

Bible Stories that Relate to a Mini-Crisis

● **The lights go out**—Jesus heals the blind man; Jesus is the Light of the world.

● **It's raining cats and dogs**—God protects Noah and the animals.

● **There's a building fire visible (not your building, of course)**—The three friends in the fiery furnace.

● **The service is running late (again) and all the kids are "starved"**—God provided manna in the wilderness (as you offer kids the saltines from your Emergency Kit)

Many of us grew up in churches where we had little or no fun. Is that how we'll be able to keep our children in church and growing in their relationships with the Lord? Have fun. Laugh, smile and enjoy the Lord and your kids. You can still have and hold boundaries for your class while you're enjoying one another and your time together.

Which situation would most likely affect kids in a positive manner? Which will bring them hurrying back next week?

One? On the first day, the teacher greets each child at the door with a nod and smile. He instructs the children to find a chair, begin coloring a Bible picture, and use only a whisper voice.

Two? On the first day, the teacher, dressed as a Bible character from that week's story, greets each child with a huge smile and a hug. He introduces himself (his character's name and his real name) and asks the child's name. He invites the child to join the other children who are in the process of building a temple out of stones (paper-filled grocery bags). This temple will become part of the set used to introduce the Bible story later that morning. The first child that arrived was given the position of "Greeter" and introduces this child to all the others.

Which would you prefer, even as an adult? The second situation involves relationship with the teacher and the other kids. It provides the kids immediate ownership in their classroom (they're in charge of the set). They see first-hand that they will play an essential role in their classroom (as they see that a child is responsible to introduce everyone) and they are immediately and actively involved in the learning process.

Unfortunately, the first situation is typical. It's what "we've always done." It's time to break out of the mold. When those kids turn 24, will they remember the coloring sheet or making a temple out of stones?

Getting to know a bunch of new kids on the first day can be daunting, but it's not insurmountable if you have the right strategies.

Be personable. Smile. Enjoy the fact that you've been chosen to lead these kids into a deeper relationship with the Lord.

Introduce yourself immediately, using the name you want them to call you. Ask them their names, and use their names frequently.

Once all the kids have arrived, gather them in a group.

Sit on the floor, slip off your shoes and invite them to do the same. Wiggle your toes. Talk about the fact that you would like this class to be like a family—one where you can be yourself, enjoy your time together, and grow closer to God.

Share some things about yourself before you ask anything of them. This will show that you really want to get to know them and hope that they'll get to know you as well. Tell them about your own family. Share with them something you hope to do someday. Tell them the thing that yucks you out the most (would that be wet worms or stinky tennis shoes?). Tell them something funny or embarrassing that happened to you when you were their age.

Open the floor to them. Ask questions and let each child share in turn. If what they share is funny, laugh. If what they share is sorrowful, comfort them. Find out something special about each child that very first day. What do they like to do? What scares them? What would they like to do for the Lord—not when they "grow up," but right now.

☼ Share with them that in order to have a great family feeling in your classroom, you'll need guidelines. Allow them to share their ideas of appropriate expectations. (Have some in mind yourself.) Usually one guideline for every two years of age is appropriate. Here are some examples.

- *Treat others as you want them to treat you.*
- *Use words that make others feel good, not bad.*
- *When someone else is speaking, listen carefully.*
- *Be considerate of others.*

Share your expectations, then invite kids to add a couple of their own. Let kids write and decorate a sign for each guideline.

☼ Talk briefly about what you'll expect when one of these rules is not followed. Keep in mind that consequences should fit the circumstances. Don't have a child stand in a corner for accidentally spilling her juice.

- *If it spills, clean it up.*
- *If it breaks, repair it (or replace it).*
- *If you say something mean, say two nice things.*
- *If you run, you'll have to sit for a while.*
- *If you speak too loudly, you'll have to whisper.*
- *If you make someone smile, you'll feel great.*
- *If you choose to be helpful, you'll feel proud.*

♡ ♡ ♡ ♡ ♡ ♡ ♡ ♡ ♡ ♡ ♡

Be Prepared

If you could predict where the roadblocks were, they wouldn't be roadblocks. You would plan differently and avoid the obstacle. But you can't always know what's going to change your plan—extra kids, a sick child, a long sermon, an absent classroom helper, your own illness. Well-laid back-up plans give you confidence that you can handle whatever comes up. For starters:

☑ *Always have one or two extra of everything.*

☑ *Become friends with the copy machine.*

☑ *Always have your emergency kit handy (see below).*

☑ *Keep abreast of fun projects by regularly scanning magazines and books.*

☑ *Know where supplies are kept.*

☑ *Pre-arrange for a teacher-pal (see below).*

☑ *Prepare for the lesson well before Saturday evening.*

☑ *Remember this phrase: "The secretary runs and knows everything."*

I've Been Down This Road Before

What speedbumps and roadblocks have you already encountered during your involvement with children's ministry? List some situations where a back-up plan would have been helpful.

Emergency Kit

What can you do when you need a fast answer? A quick solution to an unexpected situation? With 13 children clinging to your ankles or scaling the walls, you have no time to develop a plan that's optimum. Yet you don't want to waste precious minutes just filling time while you take care of something unexpected. **Assemble an emergency kit and keep it handy.** Include these items.

☑ A class set of a fun worksheet

☑ A music CD or cassette

☑ A short Christian video

☑ A set of spare clothing (sweats work great)

☑ An index card with important phone numbers and parents' names

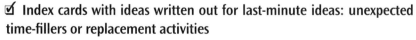

☑ Index cards with ideas written out for last-minute ideas: unexpected time-fillers or replacement activities

☑ A substitute folder (see below)

☑ Enough saltine crackers to last through a four-hour sermon

Substitute Folder

Susan ran a reasonably well-ordered class of 10 younger elementary children. Things were rough in the fall, but she quickly established class routines and expectations, and the classroom became an amiable place to be on Sunday mornings. In March, Susan needed to miss four Sundays in a row. She lined up substitutes and made sure they had teaching material. Upon her return, Susan was greeted with mayhem. Class routines were non-existent. Kids were bouncing off the walls. Yes, a substitute folder would have been a good idea.

A substitute is not just an adult body in the room when you can't be there. You still want kids to learn. Put together a folder that makes it easy for any substitute to step into your classroom and teach effectively. Include things like:

- Names of the children expected or enrolled
- Blank name tags
- Procedures or routines the kids are used to
- Health notes or special-needs notes for particular children
- Lesson materials and pertinent notes
- Location of supplies

It's a Dark, Lonely Road

What items do you have that you could keep in an "emergency kit" for those times when you need a quick change in plans? Make a list.

- Emergency kit instructions
- Index card with your phone number (so everything can be returned)
- Usual time line for phases of the lesson
- Name of your teacher-pal and where to find him or her
- General rules or expectations for the class

Last-Minute and Unexpected Time-Fillers

No matter how meticulously you calculate the flow of your lesson, there will be times when you need a meaningful activity to fill an extra few minutes. Often you can tie a last-minute activity to the story you're studying that week. Or you can innovate with a quick service project. Keep these ideas on cards in your emergency kit:

☼ Make a mosaic of the story using torn pieces of construction paper and glue.

☼ Have small groups pantomime their favorite Bible story; the rest of the class guesses the story.

☼ Hold scriptionary races. Pair the kids; tell the "drawers" a Bible story to draw; they run back to their partner and draw; the first pair to correctly get the answer gets one point.

☼ Play a CD or cassette; respond to the Lord in song and movement.

☼ Take a nature walk.

☼ Clean up the church grounds and parking lot.

☼ Watch a short Christian video.

Street Lights

A well-prepared substitute folder can make it or break it for the sub who feels like she's stumbling around in the dark. What needs to be in your substitute folder?

Supplies to gather:

Notes to make:

Pre-Arrange for a Teacher-Pal

Ideally, your teacher-pal would be with you in the classroom. If you need to leave the classroom, there's a parent or helper to look after the kids. But that's not possible in every situation. You might run into situations where you need another adult's help.

● *Find one teacher nearby who will cover your class during short emergencies. Agree to cover his or her class as well. This might mean combining classes for part of the time.*

● *If one class is older than the other, no problem. The older children become the "teacher's helpers" for the younger.*

● *Let the children know the first day of class (and remind them thereafter) what they are to do during a brief "emergency" if you need to leave (such as when Freddy loses his breakfast).*

♡ ♡ ♡ ♡ ♡ ♡ ♡ ♡ ♡ ♡ ♡

Too Few Supplies and Too Many Kids

As you gain experience teaching, you are better able to predict when time fillers will be needed. Expecting the unexpected helps prepare you for it. *List some situations where you have found yourself filling time in class recently.*

How can you make time-fillers meaningful learning or relational time?

If more kids come to your class than you're prepared for, that's a good problem! And it doesn't have to mean disaster for your careful planning. Here are some easy ideas to handle more kids than you have supplies for.

☼ Pair or group the kids to work on a project together.

☼ Let half the class work on one project while the other class does something else; switch midway through class time.

☼ Let half the class work on a project today, the other half next week. Then carry through with offering the activity the next week.

☼ Send an aide out to beg, borrow and scrounge while you lead praise and worship.

☼ Drop the original project; supplement with an activity from the last-minute idea cards in your emergency kit, and tailor it to that week's Bible story.

☼ Pray earnestly for the supplies to multiply and expect a miracle.

Walk the Road Together

Make a plan for a teacher-pal arrangement with someone in a classroom near yours.

Who can be my teacher-pal?

What arrangements do we need to make in advance?

Special Needs Friends

Everyone learns in different manners. Learning styles can be auditory (what you hear), visual (what you see), tactile (what you touch) and kinesthetic (how you move). Using children's ministry materials that consistently address a variety of learning styles will help you meet the needs of every child in your room.

Special needs come in a variety of shapes and forms. Some are clearly visible, some are hidden. Be on the lookout for "hidden" and not-so-hidden signs that may indicate a child has special needs. These signs include:

- Excessive thirst
- Perpetual need to visit the restroom
- A brief period where the child "phases out" or daydreams then does not recall what just happened
- Habitually reverses letters (especially in upper grades)
- Anti-social behaviors
- Constant fidgeting and movement
- Extremely brief attention span
- Disproportionate anger and/or outbursts
- Unreasonable bouts of crying
- Does not speak
- Language that echoes what others say
- Repetitive motions such as rocking or flapping hands
- Unreasonable jealousy
- Has no friends (poor social skills)
- Does not respond to loud sounds
- Asks for things to be repeated often
- Unexplained bruising or frequent injuries
- Extremely fearful
- Recoils at touch
- Extremely poor posture
- Unexplained limps or gaits
- Squints to read or see
- Eyes do not "align" when looking at something
- Speech impediment not related to age
- Poor memory—short- or long-term
- Poor fine or gross motor skills compared to most others the same age

Kids are quick to pick up on special needs issues. The challenge is to help them learn to be compassionate and friendly, not offended and standoffish. If it's appropriate, explain to the kids what type of special needs their friend has (or let their friend explain her own needs). Give them concrete examples of how they can help or encourage that child. Also, give them concrete examples of what not to do. You may find that the kids begin to "fight" over who gets to be their friend's helper that day. If that's the case, make a sign-up chart.

Usually you'll find one or two kids who do an exceptional job reaching out to a special-needs child. Use their gifts and strengths to your advantage. Help them teach the other kids what to do and how to act. With inclusion of special needs kids in the regular classroom becoming common in the public school systems, most children are familiar and comfortable with special-needs children. They may even have suggestions for you.

♡ ♡ ♡ ♡ ♡ ♡ ♡ ♡ ♡ ♡ ♡

Anticipating the Speedbumps

Obviously you can't always produce more copies of a four-color student handout or an ongoing class project. But you can anticipate basic supply needs.

What supplies are the first-pick of the kids? Crayons or markers? Glue stickers or school glue? Glitter glue or stickers? Watch their choices, then stock up on what they choose most often.

When Saturday Spills into Sunday

So…yesterday was a disaster.

After waiting until Saturday to prepare your lesson (time to read Chapter 3 again), the rains came, the basement flooded, and you spent the day mopping up.

Or the flu bug came and bit your child—and you spent the day mopping up.

Or unexpected company arrived, and you prepared a big meal, and spent the evening washing up.

What to do on Sunday morning? **Here's a FIRST AID KIT:**

Grab your Bible   **4 bath towels**   **4 clothespins**

As you drive to church, pray for your children, and for your peace of mind. (Don't try this *every* Sunday, but occasionally your class will love it.)

Use the Bible story for the morning—or if it is unfamiliar to you, choose one you know well. Use the story from last week. It will be a great review. Every Bible story has at least two characters in it. Ask for volunteers to play two parts. Attach two bath towels (one in front and one in back) at the shoulders with the clothespins. One size fits all, from preschool to high school.

Ask the volunteers to act out the story as you read it aloud from the Bible. When they have finished, others will want a turn. Read the story again. By that time the class will know the story well enough to do "improv." Continue to offer opportunities to act out the story, encouraging dramatic voices and characterizations. Others in the class can become the additional characters. Let the children trade parts until each has had a chance to play every part. As the class becomes involved in the story, questions will emerge that will make great discussion material. The children will never forget that story.

Think of the great dramas you might have:

• Abraham & Lot	• Jesus & Zacchaeus
• David & Saul	• Jesus & the Rich Young Ruler
• David & Goliath	• Jesus & Peter
• Naomi & Ruth	• Paul & Silas
• Daniel & Darius	• Mary & Elizabeth

When All Else Fails

A story is told of a teacher who so lost control in his classroom, that to gain his kids' attention he stood atop the desk, stomped his feet and screamed. Yes, he gained their attention. But the outcome was far different than what he anticipated. One of his students was overheard near the end of the year saying, "We thought it was so funny when he stood up on the desk. We tried all year to get him up there again." Hmm.

Every teacher will experience times when the classroom management techniques fail. Too many factors influence the nature of the classroom and the physical and emotional reactions of kids. The simplest change in the weather can cause a hurricane-force disruption in the kids. Don't limit yourself to one method for keeping kids on track with the lesson—especially if it doesn't seem to be working at the moment. Get comfortable with activities that are loud and active. Quiet rooms do *not* ensure learning.

Try using a simple signal that tells the kids they need to tone it down a bit. Try something unique and different such as a bell, a kazoo, a bird whistle, one line from a song, a long, colorful ribbon, a special clapping rhythm that kids repeat, a certain signal that kids see and pass on.

Don't be afraid to completely stop an activity if you see things spinning out of control. Quietly tell the kids that they are not handling the activity, as you would like them to. Tell them that you will try again next week. (Make sure you try again next week.) Send them to a more tranquil activity and do not let anyone return to the original activity. When the kids see you're serious and hold true to your word, you won't have to do it very often (if ever again).

Can you predict the day when the markers will dry out? When you'll have 50 percent more kids than usual? When a child will be cranky and take out a bad night's sleep on the whole class? When a teacher will not show up and forget to call anyone? No. But you can be flexible and adaptive with supplies and activities. You can remember that the relationship you're building with your kids will have for more impact than getting through every shred of lesson content.

God can turn your worst moments into your best ones. He hears those quick prayers for help. Smile, trust, pray, go with the flow and smile some more. Don't let a little (or big!) speedbump stop you from having a wonderful day ministering to children!

9 Discipline is NOT a Four Letter Word

Five-year-old Caleb whips four markers across the room before his teacher—who's sitting right next to him—can restrain his throwing arm.

Whap! They hit the side of the bookcase. One, two, three, four! Bright-eyed Josh gleefully leaps up to join the action. It looks like more fun than the activity at the table! With his face pinched between the teacher's fingers, Caleb solemnly promises not to throw any more. But behind his back he's pressing an uncapped red marker against the table. "Watch what happens," he says, grinning. The marker rockets into the air and leaves a long red streak on Michelle's cheek. Michelle wails and flails. The rest of the class bursts into laughter.

It's five minutes into class and the teacher wonders: **What have I gotten myself into and HOW DO I GET OUT?**

Who, Me?

If you sit down with a group of teachers, the topic usually turns to discipline. Kids will be kids, after all. And we teachers are definitely outnumbered! Does every week need to be a tug of war for control of the class? Not if you're discipline-smart. Think of this chapter as your classroom management toolbox. Where shall we begin? With you! A smooth running, cooperative classroom involves your behavior just as much as your kids'.

As you teach, your personality and attitudes will be on display. Let's take a moment to assess your personal style.

> **Think for a moment. What kind of animal would you be?**
>
> **Turtle**—I tend to tuck from confrontation. I like floating along and not rocking the boat.
>
> **Chameleon**—I'm easy going and will go with the flow.
>
> **Raccoon**—I set things up for fun, and encourage kids to explore the options I've provided.
>
> **Duck**—All my ducks need to be in a row and quacking when I need them to quack.
>
> **Mama Bear**—I expect kids to do what I say when I say it.

If you checkedstatements near the end of that list, your style tends toward power based authority. In class, you might inadvertently communicate this attitude: "I'm the all-knowing teacher and you're the child and don't you forget it!" Make sure you don't sacrifice the needs of the kids to meet your own need for control.

If you checked statements near the beginning of the list, you're a people pleaser, someone who might tend to look for validation from your students. You might be giving kids the message: "Will you please be my friend? I need you to like me." You need to guard against seeking approval and do what you know is best for the class.

While no one style is right or wrong, teachers who build good relationships with their kids tend to fall somewhere in the middle. And with good reason. We're teachers, but we're also learners. We're not bastions of perfection, but co-pilgrims on a spiritual journey. As disciplers, guides and mentors we need to communicate to kids that we haven't "arrived." While we're further down the road in our spiritual journey than our students, we still sit at the feet of Christ and learn from him. When humility and leadership go hand-in-hand, kids somehow become cooperative and eager to please. *Ain't that somethin'!*

> 66 *To remind kids that God is present in the classroom, light a scented votive candle before the start of each class and blow it out when class is over.* 99

The Four C's: Competent, Compassionate, Connected, Controlled

When you're in a classroom full of kids, you need to have these four qualities going for you.

✳ ✳ ✳ Be Competent ✳ ✳ ✳

Knowing "a little" about your lesson is never enough. The better prepared you are, the more you'll be able to focus on the kids and head off discipline problems before they develop. Check out Chapter 3 for great ideas on how to nail your lesson preparation early in the week.

Say goodbye to the "sit still and listen" strategy that was the hallmark of your grandmother's Sunday school (or even yours!). Provide a sensory-rich, hands-on lesson that grabs kids' hearts and minds and puts their high energy levels to good use. When kids are motivated and engaged in learning, discipline problems disappear. When kids are bored and don't see the value of what they're learning, you're inviting disaster.

> I thank my God every time I remember you. In all my prayers for all of you, I always pray with joy because of your partnership in the gospel from the first day until now, being confident of this, that he who began a good work in you will carry it on to completion until the day of Christ Jesus.
>
> Philippians 1:3–6

Set up a win-win situation in your class by teaching kids the way God made them to learn. Provide options that appeal to every learning style. Give kids variety, surprises and a balance of thoughtful and lively activities. Let them explore, discover, take ownership and you'll be delighted with the expanded attention spans that result. Cooperative students will suddenly replace the rowdy, inattentive kids you once knew. An ounce of internal motivation is worth a truckload of external control.

Rid your class time of low-priority, low-yield time wasters. Endless crossword puzzle sheets and fill-in-the blank exercises may keep kids quiet and busy, but they're effective with just one kind of learner. Make sure you do something that touches every child in the class. Create classroom experiences that are loaded with relevance to kids' everyday lives. Capture kids' imaginations and illuminate the Bible truth with stimulating sense-sational activities.

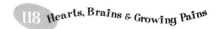

☼ ☼ ☼ Be Compassionate ☼ ☼ ☼

It's easy to look back on our childhood years with a warm sense of nostalgia. But if you could, would you want to go back to childhood? You'd give up control in most areas of your life. You'd live in a world of giants. Your lack of perspective and life experience would make problems seem permanent and insurmountable. If you watched cartoons and wrestle-mania, you'd have a lot to unlearn from our culture. There would be bullies and growth spurts and measles and you'd have to relearn long division!

Teachers who have a real heart for kids are keenly aware of the struggles of childhood. Think back to when you were a child. How did you react in a classroom when you were

Bored? _____

Hungry? _____

Tired? _____

Irritated? _____

From a child's perspective, adults nearly always operate from a position of power. For that reason, we can intimidate and humiliate without ever meaning to do so. The result? Embarrassment, helplessness, even rage. **Jesus exhibited a gentle, loving demeanor with children. Make him your model.**

Your students are looking to you for love and acceptance—even the really-hard-to-love ones! When kids act out, it's very seldom aimed at you. Look for the cause behind the behavior. First, kids' brains are wired differently from yours. Children have a need to move, so silliness and giggles are normal. So is their need for attention. If your students aren't hanging breathlessly on your every word, don't take it personally. Take a deep breath, make yourself relax, then assess the situation.

☑ Is Bill tired or hungry or simply having a bad morning?

☑ Is Jodi feeling overwhelmed or under appreciated?

☑ Was there tension between Dawn's mom and dad on the way to church?

☑ Is Dick coming down with a cold ?

☑ Did brother #1 and brother #2 spill orange juice on Lois's jumper? Again?

☑ Was the sermon just before class especially long and boring and not very "kid-friendly"?

☑ Is Susan just being goofy?

Any of these factors have a major impact on a child's ability to focus and cooperate in class. Your sensitivity and understanding can help kids get over these bumps in the road. There is no need to be an amateur psychologist or feel you must diagnose behavioral problems. **Love and concern are universal healers.** And we can supply them abundantly to our kids because our gracious God first shared them with us.

> 66 *If you feel that you are "stuck with the kid" for an hour, she probably feels the same about you!* 99

If you've ever worked with a hyperactive child, you know what it's like to have the boundaries of your compassion stretched. Kids who face a variety of learning challenges can take a lot of your energy. It's only natural for your resentment to build. Here's an important perspective-giver: *it feels worse to be inside that child than it does to be his or her teacher.* These simple strategies can be lifesavers when you're dealing with kids who can't stop moving.

☑ Use proximity control. Keep the child close to you. Use a calming touch on the shoulder or elbow.

☑ Provide something to keep hands busy. A koosh ball or squeezable ball to manipulate provides a safe, non-distracting outlet for movement.

☑ Let the child be your helper. Let him do simple classroom tasks that burn energy and save steps for you.

☑ Use her name in positive ways to help her refocus. "Jaymee, can you tell me what you're supposed to be doing now?"

☑ Commend good behavior whenever you can. Imagine the number of negative messages this child receives throughout the week.

☑ Talk to Mom or Dad about the strategies that they've found successful to keep their child on task.

☑ If you've tried all these things and still feel hamstrung by managing this child's behavior, get help. **Pair the hyperactive student with another student who has a steadying effect.** If you need to, ask a parent to stay in class as your helper.

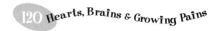

☀ ☀ ☀ Be Connected ☀ ☀ ☀

Your ability to impact kids' lives is directly related to the depth and quality of the relationships you share. Make positive connections and positive impressions. Each week, leave the busyness of preparation long enough to give every child who enters your class a warm, sincere greeting. **Call them by name.** If you're name challenged, make it a class project to create nametag necklaces. Or print out nametags in fun typefaces on a computer. Cover them with clear plastic adhesive or slip them into nametag holders. Make this your first point of connection.

> 66 *Classrooms*
> ● *are crowded*
> ● *places with lots*
> ● *of room for God's*
> ● *love.* 99

Pray for each child every week, without fail. Make sure your lesson plan includes a time to listen to kids' concerns and praises. Give them opportunities to write or draw prayer requests they don't feel comfortable sharing out loud. As you pray for kids, consider walking behind them and touching each one on the shoulder. This takes just a few moments, but the impact on kids' lives will last a lifetime.

Send kids a brief follow-up e-mail or post card.

Choose resources that emphasize a relationship-building time with your kids. And put that time right up front in your lesson. Can you just hear a freckle-face child saying this? "Why should I care about the dumb ole' lesson if the teacher doesn't care about

> *Dear (child's name),*
>
> *Thanks for letting me pray for you this week. I wrote your concern about (mention the prayer request) on a slip of paper that I keep in my Bible, and I'm praying about that every day. I just thought you'd like to know.*
>
> *Your friend and teacher, (your name)*

me?" Why, indeed? Building a connection between kids' lives and what you're about to teach makes a world of difference. You've established relevance, a natural motivator, and you've set a context of positive caring. So now your kids' brains are all "lit up" and ready to learn. Not a bad investment of time!

Let kids know why you've chosen to teach. Tell them what you like about being in children's ministry. They'll be glad to know that you're a kid at heart and that you think what happens in kids' classes is exciting and fun.

You might share a humorous story from your teaching experience, or tell about a teacher you really liked when you were a child. Tell the kids that you want them to be team players and that your goal is to make your time together something they'll look forward to every week. Your enthusiasm will be contagious!

While you're making connections, don't avoid the difficult kids. Go out of your way to establish warm, personal contact early in class with kids who tend to be disruptive. Lots of kids act out because they want attention, and negative attention is better than none at all. You'll head 'em off at the pass when you start class by supplying the positive attention they hunger for.

Kids crave leadership and boundaries, even if they act like they don't!

☀ ☀ ☀ ## Be Controlled ☀ ☀ ☀

There will be days when you'll need to stop and check your attitude at the door. Days when family or work relationships are strained, you're not feeling well, and you know your temper is simmering just below the surface.

Before you take on a classroom full of kids, pause to pray. Ask God to fill you with grace and help you overcome your "mood du jour." Your kids are counting on you to be faithful, fair and in control.

Here are some simple steps you can take to reduce your frazzle factor and stay in control on those not-so-great days.

☺ **Nab a friend from an adult class to sit in and be your helper. Say, "Hey, Nancy, I'm not really feeling on top of things today and I could use a hand with my class. Would you be willing to join me as a helper today?"**

☺ **Keep extra children's materials and classroom supplies on hand for guests and last minute brainstorms.**

☺ **Practice the discipline of keeping your voice quiet and calm.**

☺ **If you feel close to losing it, inform kids, "I'm not in such a good place right now. I'm going to take a 30-second time out." Kids will be impressed with your honesty and positive example.**

☺ **Avoid intimidating stances. Depending on the age level you teach, you're probably quite a bit larger than most of your kids. Don't get in a child's face or back a child into a corner or against a wall.**

When a conflict arises, you can stay in control by giving choices rather than ultimatums. "Andrew, our classroom rule says one person speaks at a time. You can stop talking and remain with the group, or you can visit the time out corner. Then when you're ready, you can rejoin our activities." This approach maintains Andrew's dignity and creates a win-win situation.

Use these guidelines when you give choices.

- Use the child's name.

- State the classroom rule.

- I need you to stop…(state the specific behavior).

- Give a reasonable choice that is well defined in space (where) and time (how long). To sit out in the hallway for the rest of the class time may not be reasonable, especially if there's no one supervising the hall area!

•Wrong phrasing:

"Mark, If you do not sit down then you can go to time out." This is not a choice statement.

• Correct phrasing:

"Mark, I need you to sit down. You can sit in the red chair or the blue chair or go to the time out corner until you are ready to join us again. The choice is yours."

- If a child doesn't cooperate and make an appropriate choice, give an "I care" message. "Mark, we really want you to be a part of our class." Or, "I can see that you're getting frustrated."

- Restate the choice. "You can either sit in the chair or go to time out."

- Take the choice away. "I will give you to the count of three to choose or I will choose for you." Then count to three in a controlled voice. In most cases the child will make a choice before you get to three, but be prepared to take action.

Children who are given choices will generally take the choice that benefits them the most. If class is interesting, they won't want to be left out. But by making the choice to stay, they're also choosing to abide by the rules you've created together.

In the "olden days," many teachers maintained order through negative control. The teacher's temper was something to be feared. Now we understand that negative control produces negative emotions. If a teacher yells or uses shame and blame, children internalize those negative emotions. Children who systematically experience criticism learn to feel unworthy of love.

> 66 *Do to others what you would have them do to you.* 99

Good discipline needs to be calm and non-critical. It lets kids know that you are in control and are not threatened by disruptive behavior. Setting and maintaining well-defined boundaries and offering choices helps children develop a system of inner controls, a guidance system of sorts, that will help them remember what to do and what not to do the next time their behavior takes a dip. Healthy discipline keeps a child's sense of self-worth intact.

> 66 *A child's*
> ● *spirit is*
> ● *moldable:*
> ● *Shape it, don't*
> ● *break it!* 99
> ●

Eleven Keys to Classroom Management

Approach your classroom with realistic expectations. Things aren't going to be perfect. And perfect doesn't matter anyway. Your goal is not to teach a flawless lesson, but to go for the Godprint, remember? Kids are going to be the active, curious, imaginative little people God made them to be. Hurray!

1. **Let kids participate in creating classroom rules.** Do you remember a country that was born amidst tea parties in a harbor and cries of "Taxation without representation"? The same principle applies with elementary-age kids. They'll be much more willing to cooperate with rules they've had a "say" in formulating.

2. **Once you've agreed on standards of conduct, be clear and consistent in enforcing them.** Kids have an incredible need for things to be just and fair.

> *There is no fear in love. But perfect love drives out fear, because fear has to do with punishment. The one who fears is not made perfect in love.*
> 1 John 4:18

3. **Make sure your kids are comfortable.** If it's too hot or cold, contact your facilities person. If your room has a musty smell, bring in vanilla potpourri.

4. **Use humor in large doses.** In classroom discipline, humor is your best friend. It is the antidote to confrontation, which is your worst enemy. If you find yourself in a difficult situation, defuse it with humor and grace.

- *Cross your eyes and make a weird face.*
- *Drop your mouth open and slap your hands on your cheeks.*
- *Pinch your nose and say "Now what?"*
- *Adopt a French accent and say, "Oh, peecklejuice! What eez zees?"*
- *Do your best imitation of your favorite cartoon character.*
- *Keeping a perfectly straight face, flare your nostrils several times.*

- *Push your nose up and snort.*
- *Drop a funny line from a currently popular commercial.*

Work on your comic side in front of a mirror. That bubble of humor will help you bounce right through sticky situations.

5. With younger children, use a puppet friend to drop little reminders about behavior. Even though you're connected at the hand, kids will jump to cooperate with a prompt from the puppet.

6. Meet parents when they drop off and pick up their children. Introduce yourself with a warm handshake. Let them know how much you want to support their efforts to guide their children's faith journey. A positive relationship with parents allows you to chat with them in a non-threatening way about what motivates their children to stay positively involved.

7. Get the wiggles out! When kids are wired and you find yourself spending more energy managing unruly behavior than teaching, stop everything and work the wiggles out so kids can refocus. Here are some wiggle busting techniques to get you started—you can probably think of several more.

- **Take a shake break. Have everyone stand up and shake an arm, shake a leg, then the other arm and other leg. Shake your head. Shake hands over your head, then shake hands down by your toes. Shake everything at once. Keep going until kids are breathless! Then sit down, take three deep, slow breaths and return to the lesson.**
- **Sing a song with motions. Keep a tape, CD or songbook nearby.**

- **Present a challenge to the class! Have a count off; give each child a number and see how quickly the class can count off. Each child shouts out his or her number in order and starts doing 10 jumping jacks as soon as the number is shouted.**
- **Music can be a wonderful way to tone things down, to soothe the wild beast or to fire up the brain cells. Have different kinds of music on hand. Stay away from the use of music that has wave sounds, or you will see a dramatic increase in the use of the bathroom!**

8. Make a stoplight for your classroom with green, yellow and red paper circles. This can help children visualize whether noise level or behavior level is on target or not. You can do this two ways depending on the needs of your classroom. You can use it as a way to monitor the whole classroom using one marker. Place the marker on the appropriate color of the noise level or behaviors being exhibited. Or you can use it to monitor individual children using clothespins with each child's name written on the clothespin. All children start by being clipped to the green light. Clothespins are moved to either the yellow for borderline "get-it-back-together behavior" or red "let's-have-a-chat" behavior.

9. **Set up a marble jar to catch them being good.** Every time the class or an individual behaves appropriately, announce the specific behavior you're affirming and drop a marble into a glass jar. When the jar is full, reward the class with a popcorn party!

10. **Write a word on the board that's related to the Bible story.** You might write, "loving." Erase one letter at a time for inappropriate classroom behavior. If there are any letters left at the end of class, reward the class.

11. **If talking out of turn behaviors begin to escalate, challenge kids to "be the teacher."** On a board draw a smiley face and a frowny face. Tell the class you are the smiley face because you will probably win and they are the frowny face because they will probably lose. Explain that every time someone talks out of turn, you get a point. If they are appropriate and raise their hands, they get a point. Use tally marks to indicate points. At the end of class, tally the points and declare the winner.

There is a lot of debate in the Christian Education community about the effectiveness of using tangible rewards. Many teachers and leaders use candy, privileges and certificates as external rewards for good behavior or achieving goals. Some claim that such rewards cheapen the real reward—the joy of learning. Our ultimate goal is for kids to learn because they want to, because they enjoy the growth and feeling of mastery and the achievement of conquering the wiggles and cooperating in class. No one is going to disagree with those goals.

But there are those kids who just aren't mature enough to pull themselves into line without some form of external motivation. (Think about yourself for a moment— would you do your job if there were no paycheck?) Occasionally, external rewards can be a good thing. However, if they're emphasized so they become the child's focus, that's a good indication of overuse. And if they make kids at other age levels openly jealous, that's a detriment as well.

Use external rewards wisely and sparingly. They can give the needed motivational boost from time to time. But your ultimate goal is for kids to cooperate in class because they love learning and they love God.

What to Do When a Child Acts Out

Maybe you'll never have a child grow so disruptive that you'll have to call him or her aside. But just in case you do, it's nice to have a plan you can put into motion.

• Invite the child to speak with you out of earshot of the other children. Speak quietly. Your calm demeanor will help the disruptive child gain control.

• As you state the problem, be firm, fair and state the specific behavior. Avoid the words "always," "never" and "you." Use statements like **"Anyone** I see throwing markers…." **"I need** to keep all the children safe; put the scissors down…." **"We** all sit at group time."

• Give choices. Explain that the options are to cooperate or take a time out. A time out involves sitting quietly in a designated space until the child feels he or she can rejoin the class with a positive attitude.

• Have the child state his or her choice. Every child needs the freedom to make choices, then live with the consequences. Eventually children will see that their behavior is the problem, not you or their classmates.

• Return to the other children and continue your teaching with lots of enthusiasm. The child who's sitting out will want to rejoin the fun.

• At the end of class, be sure the child knows his or her slate is clean and you're looking forward to a good time together next week.

• In exceptional situations a child may need to be removed from the room. Arrange with another teacher in the next classroom to take your class or to help out when you need it. Discuss this before a crisis occurs.

The ultimate goal of discipline is to build self-discipline, that inner control that directs positive behavior in your children even when you're not looking. Enjoy your kid-friendly class with kids vested in the work of their hands. Make positive relationships the norm in your classroom, and watch your kids aim to please you and God!

Remember, the Holy Spirit is your ever-faithful partner in the classroom. Depend on his love and power to manage your class with grace. Discipline with love the children God loves. Have fun together! Learn and be filled with God's life-giving power alongside your students—and enjoy doing it!

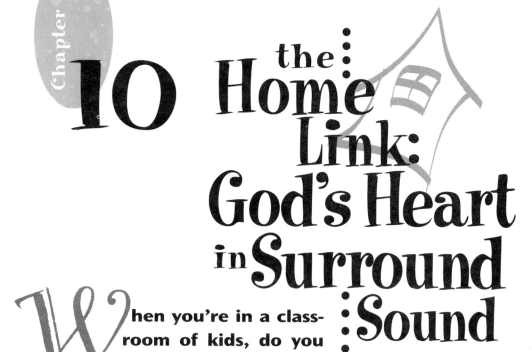

10

the Home Link: God's Heart in Surround Sound

When you're in a classroom of kids, do you sometimes feel like you're going it alone?

Like parents don't have a clue about what you're trying to teach their kids? That's not the way it's meant to be. Your Christian education program needs to be set up so that parents are on board. In fact, Scripture puts parents clearly in charge of building the foundations of their children's faith. We children's ministry workers play a supporting role.

> *These commandments that I give you today are to be upon your hearts. Impress them on your children. Talk about them when you sit at home and when you walk along the road, when you lie down and when you get up. Tie them as symbols on your hands and bind them on your foreheads. Write them on the doorframes of your houses and on your gates.*
>
> **Deuteronomy 6:6–9**

That about covers it, doesn't it? That's your day from morning to night.

The Hebrew people of the Old Testament made faith a way of life. They didn't teach "religious education" to give information but to change lives. God was a part of everyday experiences of families, not just religious leaders. We don't tie phylacteries around our heads, and most of us prefer that our children *not* write on the walls. That probably includes doorframes. So how would we paraphrase Deuteronomy 6 today? How about:

> *Talk about them in the carpool and at soccer practice, at the mall and on the Internet.*

The point is the same: **the foundations of children's faith can be laid anywhere, anytime.** It doesn't just happen during one hour a week in a children's ministry program. Children spend far more time in the care of parents and extended family than they do with a children's ministry leader. We don't always know when the "teachable moments" will surprise us. As teachers and parents, we just need to be ready to respond when they do happen.

But parents are busy and typically feel ill equipped. They're ragged from long work hours, overwhelmed by never-ending housework, distracted by bank accounts that never seem to stretch far enough. If they don't go fill the gas tank right now, they can't get to work in the morning. Or if they don't go to the grocery store tonight, there won't be milk for breakfast. Much of what keeps them busy is concern for their children's welfare. When they find a few moments to focus attention on the spiritual lives of their children, they're tongue-tied. They don't know what to say or do. Some may not want to admit how little they know about the Bible. How can they teach their children what they don't know themselves? Or they feel awkward; how do you launch a conversation about salvation with your own child? When's the right time, the right age?

> 66 *Nearly two-thirds of parents (63%) said that their church should take on an increased role in assisting parents.* (Barna, 1995) 99

Good children's ministry materials will build that essential bridge between church and home that equips and enables parents to guide children on their journey of faith. Let's look at how that can happen.

♡ ♡ ♡ ♡ ♡ ♡ ♡ ♡ ♡ ♡ ♡

Partner with Parents

The road to partnering with parents is not as hard as you might think. Keep looking toward the goal—helping parents do the job God wants them to do.

• **Communicate**　　• **Empower**　　• **Relate**

Communicate

☼ Let parents know what kids have been doing and learning. Written updates, hall-way conversations, telephone calls, e-mails—choose your method and carry through.

☼ Keep parents posted about what kids will be doing or studying during upcoming weeks. Give them some quick ideas how they can talk about the same things at home, or simple activities to do together to reinforce what you've been teaching. Maybe you never get through all the material in your curriculum, anyway. Turn those leftover activities into something that helps parents carry on what you started.

☼ Open your classroom. Let parents know they're welcome to visit, even if they aren't a designated "helper." Make sure they know it's okay to stay with a child who's reluctant to be left. **Plan a simple open house, a Celebration FUNday!**—when you invite parents to come in and see all the exciting things that have been happening in your class. And let the kids do all the work!

Empower

☼ A fire starts from just a spark. You can be the spark that gets parents involved with their kids, inside the classroom as well as at home. Ask. Challenge. Take the initiative.

☼ Make suggestions for at-home activities that result in simple parenting successes with ordinary supplies and limited time. Include discussion-starter questions that help the whole family learn from the activity.

☼ Help make parent-child interaction fun. Learning about God together doesn't have to be stuffy and somber. It's joyous and festive. Give parents an alternative to the dreary family devotions that bored them stiff when they were kids.

☼ Involve parents in planning out-of-class activities for the whole class. You may be surprised how quickly they will open their backyards or volunteer their minivans. Sometimes all that's lacking is the initiative that you can supply.

☼ **Make helping in the classroom doable.** Many parents are willing. Reluctance comes from uncertainty about what the expectation is. Be specific about how they can help: pass out scissors, be a buddy to a struggling child, run the CD player.

☼ Match tasks to gifts for classroom help or class projects. Don't ask the craft-impaired parent to cut out the construction paper patterns with kindergarten-size scissors. Find out what talents parents have before you ask them to do something. Who's good at crafts? Who's good at hamming it up in a costume? Who would bring you all the cookies and punch you could ever want? Who would make your photocopies?

Relate

☼ When you welcome the child, welcome the parent. With just a moment of eye contact, you can assure a parent that a child will be well cared for. When a parent comes to pick up a child from your classroom, speak to him or her, even if you literally have just a second. **Communicate how glad you were that the child was in your class.**

☼ Listen to children. A lot goes on in their brains. They're learning every day just by interacting with their environment, and they'd love to tell you all about it. Make some time in your class hour to just listen, widen your eyes, ooh and ah at the appropriate times. Look kids in the eye when they're talking to you. Maybe you can do three other things and listen at the same time, but the child who's talking needs your full attention.

☼ **Send children out with a blessing.** The last minutes of any children's ministry program can quickly degenerate into chaos. Children are charged up from the activities, and leaders are watching the clock and perhaps rushing through the last few steps of the lesson. Regrouping doesn't have to be a major production. Develop a signal that lets kids know it's time to gather their things. Then as they go out the door, speak a simple blessing that reinforces the point you've been teaching. Let parents hear you say it. "God made you, Tess, and you're special." "God is in control; you can trust him, Michael." "Peter, keep your eyes open for the amazing things God can do for you this week."

☼ **Be a real person, not just a Sunday school teacher.** Have you ever had the experience of seeing someone who seems familiar, but you just can't quite figure out why? Then it turns out to be someone you're used to seeing behind the checkout counter at the grocery story. Seeing her out of context was a bit of a jolt, but she has a real life, too! Look for natural opportunities to connect with the kids in your class and their families outside of the classroom—sit next to them in the worship service; invite a child over to play with your own child; take your soggy plate and plop down next to them at the next church potluck. Be alert for their minivans in the discount store parking lot.

☼ **Celebrate together.** Plan special times when the kids in your class and their families can celebrate and show off what they've been learning. Let the kids act out their favorite story from the quarter for their families; or mix up a snack that will remind everyone of a Bible verse; make up a riotous review game that pits kids against their parents.

Communicate. Empower. Relate. And do all this in the real world, knowing what family life is like and what parents are up against.

Respect the real lives of parents. No guilt trips. No oughtas. No should haves. Two-income and single-parent families are a reality, not a subject for social debate. Parents work long hours and come home tired. They want to connect with their kids—and they want to succeed at it. Help them; don't get in their way. They don't want to be dodging the teacher who is asking for a bigger time commitment than they can make to prepare for a class outing. They don't want to avoid you at church because they're not doing the extra worksheets you're sending home. Ask for involvement. Expect involvement. Just be willing to accept it in whatever shape or form the parents can manage, not a predetermined one-size-fits-all method.

> For it is God who works in you to will and to act according to his good purpose.
>
> Philippians 2:13

You are God's tool in the home link. You can go to 16 different children's ministry conferences and read dozens of books that tell you everything you should be doing for a power-packed, life-transforming ministry. And you may come away overwhelmed and wondering if you're competent. Banish those thoughts! God has gifted you and called you. Focus on doing what you *can* do.

♡ ♡ ♡ ♡ ♡ ♡ ♡ ♡ ♡ ♡ ♡

Rendezvous in Cyberspace

Sandy just agreed to serve as secretary to the Christian education ministry team at her church. She's been informed that part of her responsibility is to keep the postcards and postage boxes stocked. These are on the top shelf in a closet. A teacher can go there and get a postcard and a stamp when she wants to send a card to an absent child or to acknowledge a birthday. So Sandy dutifully checks out the supplies. She finds postcards that look like they were ordered—and last used—in the late 1970s, and postage stamps that haven't been sufficient for a postcard for at least five years. She wonders if this is the best teachers can do.

Sound familiar?

How many people in the United States and Canada have Internet access?

A.) 1 in 3   B.) 1 in 4   C.) 1 in 2   D.) 1 in 5

If you said "C," you're right. And there's no reason to think that the families in your church are any different. One in two of them have Internet access in their homes.

The kids in those households might very well be the ones who go online the most. And Internet use is only going to grow. Children's ministry leaders have the opportunity to ride the information highway to reach their kids, not sit idly by while someone else reaches them first.

Kids love to get mail. CJ, a nine year old, asked her dad to help her build a wooden mailbox. She painted on a street number and hung the box on the wall outside her room with instructions that all her mail be delivered there. The eternal optimist, she had lofty visions. Grown-ups like mail, too. Think about how you felt the last time you got an envelope that didn't contain a bill or a form letter.

The postal service may be noticing a decline in first class personal mail, but that doesn't mean people aren't writing letters. It's just that more and more personal communication is happening electronically. No buying stamps. No out-of-the-way trips to a mail box. No wondering if you've missed the last pick-up for the weekend. No guessing how many days delivery will take. Will the card get there in time? You can send e-mail in your fuzzy puppy slippers in the middle of the night, when you remember a child's special birthday prayer request. You don't have to drag your toddler away from his playtime in order to mail a card and let a child in your class know you missed her. You don't have to find a photocopier or use up all your ink printing out the same message 10 times when you want to give parents an update on what's happening in your class. You don't have to write a tome. A few encouraging words can make an incredible impact on a child or a parent. Electronic clip art, fun fonts and a splash of color—most likely already in the software you have—are simple additions to your message that make it even more fun to receive.

What's so great about the Internet?

- **It's comfortable.** Kids are using computers at younger and younger ages. They can't imagine life without one!

- **It's fun.** There are a lot of way-cool sites for kids, where learning happens, imagination is empowered, and intellect is challenged.

- **It's available.** Whatever you're interested in, you can find a web site that gives you stuff to look at, think about, play with, try out.

- **It's quick.** You can find information fast.

- **It's changing communication.** You can send and receive letters at the push of a button.

- **It's convenient.** Parents have access to a world of information without having to leave the napping toddler or dinner simmering on the stove.

e-mail   Dear Ben,

I'm praying for you this week. I'm asking Jesus to make you more like him every day. If you have something special I can pray for, send me a message back!

e-mail

Dear Josh,

It's your special day! I'm so glad God created you just the way you are.

e-mail

Dear Molly,

In class I saw you helping Katie with her project. You're pretty good with glue and scissors! Did you know it makes Jesus happy when you're helpful to other people?

Solve the "Take-Home" Dilemma

Lynn sat in the quiet of the sanctuary after the worship service, waiting for her husband to come out of a brief council meeting. She nearly whimpered aloud as she looked around and saw the clutter on the chairs. Just that week she had paid the bill for the Sunday school curriculum materials for the new quarter. The clutter on the chairs represented dollars generously given by God's people, reduced in a matter of minutes to trash. All the children received a take-home paper as they left their classrooms. Lynn could see that at least a third of those papers were on the chairs and floor of the sanctuary. She could just picture another third crumpled and mud-streaked in the back seats of cars. More were stuffed into parents' Bibles. She wondered woefully how many would actually get taken out and read.

Let's Be Honest

- *How many parents in your church know if the take-home paper got home last week?*

- *How many kids can remember if they took one home?*

- *How many kids or parents have looked at the take-home in the last month? In the last six months?*

For decades, children's ministry leaders have recognized that they can come alongside parents and help with the task of helping children become disciples of Jesus. Take-home papers have been the cornerstone of this effort. Families who read them find exciting, well-written Bible stories, colorful reminders of Bible verses, games and activities to do together. But many families don't reap the benefits. In recent years, more and more children's ministry leaders have asked the question Lynn asked: Are take-homes a good use of money when they are more often "leave-behinds"?

What is a take-home, anyway? What are teachers hoping will happen when they put one in the hands of a child at the end of class? What are parents expecting when they stuff them into their Bibles with every good intention of looking at them later?

A take-home builds a natural link, a home link, between what a child experiences in a children's ministry program and how to live the way Jesus wants them to live in a real home environment. That's what the teacher hopes for. That's the kind of help the parent is looking for.

The real puzzlers are:

☼ What would encourage a child to take the take-home home?

☼ What would motivate a parent to look at it, read it, act on it?

First, look at things from a child's perspective. The teacher has just made you put your art project on the counter before you finished it and called you to the prayer circle. Time was short, so she said a quick prayer that covered anything and everything. Then on your way out the door, she pressed a paper into your hand. What you really wanted to take home was your art project. But it's not finished. Besides that, your friends are waiting. You have just a few minutes before the cars in the parking lot take off in all directions and all you can think of is getting in a game of tag before everyone's gone.

Now you're the parent, and you've met your child in the church lobby. He shoves a pile of papers at you and shoots out the door to climb the tree in front of the build-

Not a techie?

If you're not a techno-whiz, chances are you know someone who is. The species is growing astronomically. If you have a computer and Internet access but haven't quite conquered its use, ask for help. Or, if you can handle simple e-mail but would like something more sophisticated, perhaps your techie friend can help you set up a site that families in your class can access to see what's new. Better yet, perhaps you use a curriculum that provides all these things for you with the click of your mouse.

ing. You start to turn the paper right side up and look at it. Just then someone touches your elbow to ask you a question. So instead you fold it and stick it inside your Bible. Next week, when you pick up your Bible to go to church, the papers fall out. Oh, well. There will be more to take their place this week.

How can we change this picture?

What if your child carried out of the classroom a project she had been working on for several weeks and took great pride in? What if the take-home were that art project? What if she was so proud of it that she couldn't wait to tell you about it? What if it had a fun hanger so she would want to display it in the car or on her bedroom door or on the fridge? Now you have a bridge between the church and the home: a home link that won't be ignored.

Get the Take-homes Home

> ● *Think beyond paper when you plan something to send home. Who says a take-home has to be flat and rectangular?*

> ● *Think different. Kids are more likely to take home something they've invested themselves in, something that expresses their individuality, rather than a paper that looks just like everyone else's.*

> ● *Think involvement. Look for ways to involve the parents or the whole family. Use a home link that helps parents talk with and interact with their kids. Give kids the advantage: help them start the conversations that their parents would love to have.*

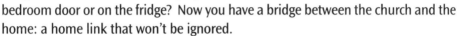

Simple Successes

If you believe in bringing Deuteronomy 6 to life, you'll want to help parents do it. How? Have a meeting? More than half your parents won't come. Send home a great book? Who has time to read it?

Don't think in terms of educating parents about what their role is. Instead, think of empowering them in the role they already know they have. Don't add to their burden; share it. Give them ways to be successful with just a few minutes at a time. No big mess, no long supply list, no complicated agenda. The resources you use should be giving you loads of ideas to pass on to parents that will give them simple parenting successes. **Here are some examples of the kinds of suggestions you'll find in Godprints.**

1. When you ask a three year old, "What did you learn about in Sunday school today?" what kind of answer do you get? That question is more complex than a lot of preschoolers can respond to. But parents want to know what their children are learning. If they have a starting place, their task is a lot easier. You can give it to them.

Send home a simple reproducible sheet that lets parents of preschoolers know what they did in your class. Something that will help them start a simple conversation with

Jesus is God's Son!
Luke 2:1–7

○ I pretended to take care of baby Jesus.
○ I spelled "Jesus" with blocks.
○ I made Jesus' name pop up.
○ I decorated a heart shaped cookie.

their three year old about what happened in Sunday school. Make sure the Bible reference is on the page.

2. Give kids a joke or a tongue twister to try out on their parents. Once they break the ice with laughter, they can ask their parents to share an experience that relates to the lesson you taught. Put both the joke and the question on slip of paper that can tuck in a pocket with a nifty hanger that can go anywhere. Kids can't resist sharing a good joke, so you can be sure the paper will be out and used before the child gets home.

• **Knock, knock.**
  Who's there?
  Juicy.
  Juicy who?
  Juicy which way Adam and Eve went?
  Where in God's creation do you feel especially close to God, the creator? How do you think God feels about his world today?

• **What did Adam call a pig with three eyes?**
  A piiig.

3. Send home or e-mail simple instructions for an easy project that can be done with ordinary household supplies. Help parents connect with their kids while doing something that the kids find interesting. Suggestions for what to say are as helpful to parents as topics to talk about.

*R*eview the story of Job. Then choose a recipe for cookies or brownies that you can make together. As you work in the kitchen, take a small taste of each ingredient before it's mixed in (except for the raw eggs). Which ones taste good and which ones taste bad? Then put the dough or batter into the hot oven. What will we get when all these things, both good and bad, are mixed together and baked? Of course the answer is "Something good to eat!"

While you enjoy eating your treat together, talk about how good and bad things in life can work together. For example, moving to a new house might seem bad at first, but it could lead to making a new friend or having your own room. Or, eating lots of candy might seem good, but it can lead to cavities or poor health. How can knowing that God loves us in both good and bad times give us a hopeful attitude?

*R*ead the story of Noah from Genesis 6–9. Get your family together for a scavenger hunt. Set your kitchen timer for 10 minutes. Then scurry around and try to find 10 things that come in pairs. Line everything up on a table like pairs of animals going into the ark. Give everyone a chance to tell about what they found. Talk about:

• Why are these things important to us?

• What do we do to take care of these things?

• How is that like the way God takes care of us?

Read the story of Mary's visit to Elizabeth from Luke 1:5–47 and 57–66. Then get out your art supplies.

Make a shimmering rainbow to remind you to trust God and never lose hope. First, write the word "HOPE" in white crayon on the center of a paper plate. Make the letters large and thick. Gently mist the plate with a spray bottle of water. The plate should be damp but there shouldn't be any puddles. With three different brushes, stir up red, yellow and blue watercolor or tempera paint until the paint is thin and watery. Drop the watery colors onto the damp plate and tip it so the colors run together and form all the colors of the rainbow! See how the word "HOPE" shines through? Decorate the edge of the plate with ribbon or glitter and hang it.

God's Love in Surround Sound

We need to surround kids with the things of God. Today's kids are used to multiple exposures. They expect to see their favorite cartoon characters on the cartons of their fast food meals or popping out of cereal boxes. A movie character shows up in a book series or vice versa. Soft toys, action figures, games and puzzles, TV programs about the same subject—all are routine for today's kids.

Parents and teachers can surround kids with God's love just as effectively. Home links that can't be folded into paper airplanes are just the beginning. Relationships at home, at church, in the community. Learning together. Real conversations. Hearing God's truths anywhere, anytime—that's God's love in surround sound. And it changes kids' lives.

Finally, brothers, whatever is true, whatever is noble, whatever is right, whatever is pure, whatever is lovely, whatever is admirable—if anything is excellent or praiseworthy—think about such things. Whatever you have learned or received or heard from me, or seen in me—put it into practice. And the God of peace will be with you.

Philippians 4:8–9

11

The Trust Factor

ell, you did it. You signed up (or were you volunteered?) to touch the lives of children in your church. No small task, that's for sure.

This job is full of significance and life-long consequences. What in the world were you thinking? Can you possibly give your students all the love and learning that they'll need? Take a deep breath and rest in the Lord. These are God's children. They're in God's care. He's just asking you to be a vessel of his love. His Word tells us exactly what he expects of us.

He has showed you, O man, what is good. And what does the LORD require of you? To act justly and to love mercy and to walk humbly with your God.

Micah 6:8

Will It Make a Difference?

Even people with long experience in children's ministry sometimes wonder if what they're doing is really making a difference in the lives of their kids. A children's pastor tells this story.

For weeks I had been speaking at the campfire every night, as groups of third, fourth and fifth graders came to church camp. Each afternoon I would take my Bible and go to the woods to prepare that evening's talk. Always I would pray, "Lord, help me to show these children who you are, how much you love them, how you sent your Son to die for each of them, how you want each of them to make the decision themselves to follow you." How carefully I planned the songs, the stories—all designed to prepare each child to hear the Gospel message. How I prayed that the Lord would give me the right illustration, the perfect words.

Late one afternoon, as I sat at the foot of a ponderosa pine on the top of a hill near the camp, I poured out my heart to God. "I have no new ideas today, Lord. I'm afraid I will bore them tonight. Please give me something wonderful to say. I want them to love you, Lord."

And then I heard the Lord speaking to me. "This isn't about *you*. It isn't *your* words, or *your* ideas, or *your* illustrations. Trust me. These are my children. I created them in my image."

I watched the sun setting over the camp. I realized I don't fear the sunset because I know God planned for the sun to rise again tomorrow. That blue jay doesn't worry about his next meal. He trusts that God will feed him. This ponderosa pine thrives because God's rain and sunshine come faithfully as needed. God was asking me to trust that he would work through me to reach the hearts of these children.

I began to praise God for all the ways I trusted him:

that he would keep my heart beating through the night, that these children would grow just as he created them to, that down the hill counselors were leading Bible studies and meeting kids' needs just as they had been trained to do. God said to me, "See, you can trust me in all these things. Trust that I want each of these children in my family even more than you do."

I prayed the words of Psalm 51:15, "O Lord, open my lips, and my mouth will declare your praise." A peace that passes understanding washed over me, as I knew that at the campfire that evening, I could speak with absolute confidence that we can trust God for everything. I was certain that God would use my words, no matter how I felt about them. It was all about him and the kids, and not about me.

We can trust God to leave his touch on each child we teach. He has created each child in his image. Jesus is our mentor. We are mentors to our children. We want them to see Jesus, not us.

God in the way God intends. It's about God imprinting on each child the traits that will make that child more Christlike.

It's about Godprints.

> You will keep in perfect peace him whose mind is steadfast, because he trusts in you.
>
> Isaiah 26:3

Godprints show what results when God is present in a child's life. This is the evidence that God was there, walking with the child through each struggle.

This is where we begin to TRUST.

We trust that God has a perfect plan for each child. We trust that he will use us to help each child discover Godprints—the touch of God that changes a child's life. We trust that these Godprints are the evidence that God is active in the child's life.

♡ ♡ ♡ ♡ ♡ ♡ ♡ ♡ ♡ ♡ ♡

A Psalm for Teachers

Are you feeling the need of a big dose of trust? Read Psalm 16. It's full of wonderful promises for those who teach children.

Lord, you have assigned me my portion and my cup.

God has planned for you to serve your church and these children. This is your portion. It is perfect because he planned it. These are the good works he planned in advance for you to do. Your "cup" is filled to overflowing. Into it he has poured all of the life experiences you have had, out of which you will teach. You can help each child discover Godprints in his or her life, because you are discovering God's pattern for your own.

You have made my lot secure.

Regardless of how the storms of life have battered you, you have been called to share with children how God is always faithful. He can always be trusted. Because our security is in the God who knows us better than we know ourselves, we can know a security the world cannot understand.

The boundary lines have fallen for
me in pleasant places.

So often we see the boundaries of our lives as limits. Oh, how we want to push against those boundaries. But when we step back and look at our lives through God's eyes, we can see how he has protected us with the boundaries he has put around us. We are not called to save the whole world, just to be faithful to those children in our class and help them discover God's touch.

Surely I have a delightful inheritance.

There is no greater calling than to teach children about Jesus and what God has planned for their lives. Praise the Lord that he has given you this holy calling. Praise him that he has equipped you to teach. Praise him that your weakness is made perfect in his strength. Praise him that you can trust him to work through you.

I have set the Lord always before me.
Because he is at my right hand, I will not be shaken.

What confidence we have when we commit our lives to the Lord. When we spend time with him each day in prayer and in reading his Word, he is in our thoughts and our words. When tough times come (and they will) we can face them with the assurance that the Lord will be with us. We will not be shaken.

Trusting the Holy Spirit to Be Your Guide

We can trust the Holy Spirit to be our guide in our teaching. The Scriptures show us so many facets of God's Holy Spirit that whatever it is we need, the Holy Spirit will provide.

The Holy Spirit Is the Spirit of Christ

The Holy Spirit is our perfect guide because Christ is the perfection that spans all of eternity. Christ always was and always will be. There is nothing you are feeling now that he has not felt. His Spirit will guide you through your preparation and study; indeed, through every moment of your life.

The Holy Spirit Is the Spirit of Counsel

When you need a counselor, call the Holy Spirit. His office is always open. His phone number is in the book of Jeremiah.

> *Call to me and I will answer you and tell you great and unsearchable things you do not know.*
>
> **Jeremiah 33:3.**

He is never too busy to listen, and understands even the thoughts you cannot express. Call on him and be amazed at the insight you will receive.

The Holy Spirit Is the Spirit of Power

Do not let your hearts be troubled. Trust in God; trust also in me.

John 14:1

If it's power you need, the Holy Spirit is ready to deliver the full power of God. That power was immense enough to create the universe and resurrect Jesus Christ from the dead. That power was made available to you at the moment of your salvation. Ask and you shall receive. Trust God's Spirit to guide you as you teach.

The Holy Spirit Is the Spirit of Faith

Faith is a gift of grace. As with any gift, it is useless until it is unwrapped. Receive this gift. And step out in faith that the Holy Spirit will guide as you teach and model Christ's love to your class. Children learn faith by watching faith in action. Ask the Holy Spirit to guide you as you tell *your* faith story to your class. They will begin to understand how precious the gift of faith is.

The Holy Spirit Is the Spirit of Grace

The gift of grace is the most difficult to receive. In a world that esteems us for what we do, it is hard to believe that it is by grace we are saved. This is the gift of God. It's not about our works. He doesn't want us to boast (Ephesians 2:8–9). Accept the grace God offers as you step into your classroom. God has saved you by grace, and it is his will and purpose to do the same for the children you teach.

The Holy Spirit Is the Spirit of Holiness

Scripture commands us to "be holy, because I am holy" (1 Peter 1:16). But it is only with the guidance of the Holy Spirit that we can begin to live a holy lifestyle. Not "holier-than-thou," but a bit holier each day as we are conformed to the image of Christ. This is a work the Holy Spirit is eager to do in your life.

The Holy Spirit Is the Spirit of Knowledge

The Holy Spirit will guide and direct us, as we are faithful to study God's Word. It is only by reading the instructional book for life that we can honestly attempt to teach his children. If you are new to the study of God's Word, press on. You can take on this daunting task bit by bit. (It takes about 85 hours to read the Bible all the way through—or 15 minutes a day for a year.) Read and pray, asking the Spirit of Knowledge to impress it on your heart.

Pick-me-up verses for future encouragement:

Deuteronomy 31:8

Joshua 1:7–9

Psalm 40:1–5

Psalm 42:5

Psalm 91:1–2

Psalm 103:8–18

Romans 8:18

Romans 8:28

Hebrews 4:14–16

John 14:27

The Holy Spirit Is the Spirit of Wisdom

Wisdom is seeing things from God's point of view. As you read and study his Word, you will begin to see life as God sees it—from an eternal perspective. This kind of wisdom will help you get your priorities in order, put first things first, major on the majors. The Holy Spirit also helps you sort out the artificial wisdom of the world and the lure of the false.

The Holy Spirit Is the Spirit of Revelation

As you prepare to teach, you will read the stories in the Bible and look for all God wants to teach you and your children. It is in this reading and studying that the Spirit of Revelation brings to your mind exactly what your children need to know for the Godprint of this particular story to imprint on their lives.

> *Trust in the Lord with all your heart and lean not on your own understanding; in all your ways acknowledge him, and he will make your paths straight.*
>
> Proverbs 3:5–6

Pray for this guidance from the Holy Spirit every time you read, study and prepare, confident that he who began a good work in you will bring it to completion.

♡ ♡ ♡ ♡ ♡ ♡ ♡ ♡ ♡ ♡ ♡

When Everything Goes Haywire

The day may come when the wheels come off, when everything you planned bombs, when the children don't seem to care a whit about class or anything you have to say. On your way home from church you may find yourself mentally composing a letter of resignation from your teaching responsibility. Or you may replay the morning in your mind, adding "if onlys" along the way:

If only...I had been better prepared today.

If only...the twins hadn't been there.

If only...the sermon hadn't gone so long.

If only...the markers hadn't been all dried out.

If only...Freddy had taken his Ritalin!

What's a teacher to do with those feelings of discouragement? Of failure? Of frustration?

There is a balm to be found in the greatest story ever told! Find a few quiet minutes to meditate on the truth of God's Word. God is faithful. You can trust him. **Gather your Bible, your journal and a steaming cup of tea or coffee.** Go to your porch or sit by a window. If it's noisy at your house, escape to the park or a cozy coffee shop. Or hide in the bathtub.

Open your Bible to Philippians, take out your journal and respond to God's Word. Hear the apostle Paul saying to you:

❄ ❄ ❄

I thank my God every time I remember you. In all my prayers for all of you, I always pray with joy because of your partnership in the gospel from the first day until now, being confident of this, that he who began a good work in you will carry it on to completion until the day of Christ Jesus.

Philippians 1:3–6

❄ ❄ ❄

Do you see how *you are in partnership with Jesus,* sharing the good news of the Gospel with the children in your class? Jesus has been there with you from your first day of teaching. It is his good work you are doing. Jesus has helped you in the past. He will help you in the future.

Don't allow yourself to dwell on down moments—there's an enemy who would be delighted to have you do that! Remember the children who were listening to the story, who did enjoy the activities, the parent who spoke a kind word. Read Paul's words thoughtfully and prayerfully:

❄ ❄ ❄

I press on to take hold of that for which Christ Jesus took hold of me. Brothers, I do not consider myself yet to have taken hold of it. But one thing I do: Forgetting what is behind and straining toward what is ahead, I press on toward the goal to win the prize for which God has called me heavenward in Christ Jesus.

Philippians 3:12–14

❄ ❄ ❄

God has placed a divine calling on your life and the lives of the children in your class. He will not allow one hectic morning to interrupt his perfect plans. You may rest in the knowledge that:

❅ ❅ ❅

God is not unjust; he will not forget your work and the love you have shown him as you have helped his people and continue to help them.

Hebrews 6:10

♡ ♡ ♡ ♡ ♡ ♡ ♡ ♡ ♡ ♡ ♡

You Never Know When You've Left a Godprint!

As the rain and the snow come down from heaven,
and do not return to it without watering the earth
and making it bud and flourish,
so that it yields seed for the sower and bread for the eater,
so is my word that goes out from my mouth:
It will not return to me empty,
but will accomplish what I desire
and achieve the purpose for which I sent it.

Isaiah 55:10–11

What a promise we have from God that his Word will not return to him empty! As we teach, we need to keep the eternal perspective. We lovingly prepare the soil, then plant each seed just so. After we have planted, we don't dig around in the dirt to see what is going on down there. We trust God to do what God does: bring life.

We're the faithful sowers. But it is God who sends the sunshine and the nourishing rains. Trust him to bring the growth.

In that day they will say,
"Surely this is our God;
we trusted in him, and he saved us.
This is the LORD, we trusted in him;
let us rejoice and be glad in his salvation."

Isaiah 25:9

12 Celebrate God's Touch

Count yourself blessed. You've been entrusted with God's most precious gift—kids.

God has chosen you to model his love in your teaching—a role which some days will make you think you deserve to be carried away by a band of angels! There will be times when you wonder if you've touched their heart and brains, and whether you'll survive their growing pains! That's why it's so important to cling to those wondrous times...

☼ when little John's eyes pop open with understanding.

☼ when Jess brings two friends to Sunday school because it's an exciting place to be.

☼ when Brittany tells you she asked Jesus to be her Savior.

☼ when the kids spontaneously encircle a visitor and make him feel as if he's been there all of his little life.

☼ when Philippe shyly gives you a hug as he leaves, his mother staring astonished at his gesture.

☼ when your entire class voluntarily learns every Bible memory verse in sign language to help make a hearing-impaired student feel included.

☼ when the class for an entire year has been praying for José's grandfather's salvation, and one day it happens.

These are the reasons we teach. Celebrate God's touch on the kids in your class!

♡ ♡ ♡ ♡ ♡ ♡ ♡ ♡ ♡ ♡ ♡

God Is at Work...

in your classroom whether you realize it or not. We have an enemy who delights in pointing out our difficult spots and little failures. Make a determined choice to focus on the positive things God is doing. Because he *is* at work!

In all my prayers for all of you, I always pray with joy because of your partnership in the gospel from the first day until now, being confident of this, that he who began a good work in you will carry it on to completion until the day of Christ Jesus.

Philippians 1:4–6

Through God's grace and the partnership of the Holy Spirit, you are leaving an indelible Godprint on the kids whose lives you touch. The evidence is not always immediate, and your impact may not take the form you expect. **This truth is wonderfully illustrated in the experience of one of our Godprints editors.** Your heart will be warmed by her story.

My degree was in early childhood, teaching kindergarten. Although my plan was to teach young children, as a safeguard I earned a double major that included teaching up to eighth grade. It was a good thing I had, because here I was, 21, fresh out of college, and staring at 30 fifth graders. Why in the world did I think I could do this? Where were the five year olds?

Looking out over that class, I heartily wished for the Lord's return!

For years I looked back on that first year of my teaching career with a heavy heart. Self-doubt and worry plagued me. Had I done more harm than good? Had I made even the slightest positive impact? Did they really know I loved them? As I blundered through 400 discipline techniques, stumbled through lessons, and fell flat on my face attempting to "positively motivate" kids, did they receive any education at all?

It wasn't until those fifth graders were old enough to be sophomores in college that God revealed to me the truth about that first year of teaching. Still teaching in the same district, I'd moved to another school and a third-grade classroom (which was much more suited to me, I must admit). At the high school graduation party of a co-worker's son, I noticed a pretty young woman chatting with the graduate. She looked familiar, but I couldn't place her. I noticed that she was watching me closely. Finally she approached me.

"Are you Ms. Weary?"

I was still nodding when she bear-hugged me. "I'm Jan. You were my fifth-grade teacher."

Everything clicked. Jan had been one of the students in my very first classroom of 30 fifth graders that nearly killed me. The classroom of 30 fifth graders that caused me to question my effectiveness. The ones I'd felt sorry for all these years because they'd been stuck with me for a teacher.

Jan sat beside me and chatted enthusiastically. "You were my very favorite teacher in all my school years! **I still have my I.C.C.M. card.**"

"Your what?" My face must have revealed complete confusion.

"You don't remember the I.C.C.M. Club? It was the coolest thing. Don't you remember the red carpet?"

Oh, yes. The red carpet. In the late 60s my parents had a room covered in bright red shag carpeting. Being the poor but industrious teacher I was, when they ripped up the carpeting, I snagged it and used it to make the classroom more "homey."

Jan continued, "Those of us who behaved and got our work done got to be members of the I.C.C.M. Club and move our desks onto the red carpet. It was so cool."

It was starting to come back to me. The I.C.C.M. Club—the I Can Control Myself Club. One of the hundreds of discipline and reward systems I had tried that year. The one that finally worked a bit.

Jan bubbled on about how I had been her favorite teacher…and how much she had learned that year…and how fun our class was…and did I know the book I read to them was now her favorite…and because of me she was thinking about becoming a teacher herself…and did I know that KP still had a crush on me until he was in high school?

Jan went on to tell me that she was involved with a Christian youth organization as she attended college. She shared with me some of the victories in her life, as well as some of the disappointments. Somehow, though, she'd always come back to, "Do you remember in fifth grade when…?"

We exchanged addresses, then parted with a huge hug. "I'll never forget you, Ms. Weary."

I don't know if Jan will ever realize what a priceless gift she gave me that evening. Thank you, Jan.

Because of you, your kids are learning to KNOW GOD.

Did you identify with this teacher's struggles? Someday you'll identify with her joy. But know this: what you're doing *right now* matters, whether you see visible results or not. Because of you, your kids are learning to know God. Because of you, they're developing a foundational understanding of God's Word that will serve them their whole lives through. Because of you, they're learning concrete ways to show Jesus' love to others. Never let yourself doubt that you're making a difference. **Consider this story from a Godprints editor.**

On the first day of teaching second grade, I arrived early to tie a helium balloon onto each child's chair. The classroom was bobbing with a rainbow of gas-filled balloons. I also added a dab of fragrant oil and pressed a heart-felt prayer into each balloon. I spent time preparing for "my kids" spiritually as well as physically. The balloons brought looks of pleasure to the kids and their parents; somehow, I felt the prayers brought pleasure to their heavenly Father. Into that classroom came two very special students: Abdul and Theresa.

The moment Abdul entered the room, I knew something was wrong. Abdul never made eye contact. He could not sit still. He preferred to stand behind his desk and rhythmically rock back and forth, back and forth. He was not able to complete the simplest task. He did not speak to others. I was outraged that this child who obviously suffered from autism was not in a class suited for his needs.

I immediately inquired about Abdul. I learned that he had been in the public school system since before he was four. Because he was from a family that spoke a language other than English, Abdul's unique behaviors were simply connected to the "English as a second language" label and never investigated.

It took me six months hounding personnel and banging on doors before Abdul was properly diagnosed and placed in a classroom designed for his needs. Although that was what I had been fighting for, releasing him was one of the more difficult things I ever did. Abdul and I had become friends. Abdul finally looked me in the eyes—even if it was for just a brief millisecond of time. Once he actually blessed me with a smile. And I'll never forget the day I heard him

 giggle with pleasure when he and I were throwing a Velcro® ball in the hallway. As he left our classroom, Abdul actually hugged me.

There is no question in my mind that the Lord used me as a vessel to touch Abdul's life. The proof was too physical—too visual—to deny. But Theresa was a different story.

Theresa came in that first day shyly. No parent led her in to help her find her seat or meet her new teacher. Theresa was probably one of the brightest children I ever taught. She caught onto things easily. And willingly, but shyly, she helped others who struggled. She never caused any trouble. She quietly did her work exceptionally well, always obeyed rules, and always did exactly what I expected.

I remember the day when I realized how unique my relationship with Theresa was. She quietly entered the room early one morning. In her hand was a thick book. Its cover displayed a childish but extensive drawing. Its many pages were filled with a typewritten manuscript and labor-intensive illustrations. Theresa had been working since school began on her first novel, and it was dedicated to me.

I still have her book. It's a treasure I'll always cherish. But I didn't know its significance until later.

At the end of the school year I received a letter from Theresa's grandfather. He explained that just days before school started, Theresa and her father were in the study when Theresa's mother walked in, announced she no longer loved either of them and was leaving. Months later, the same mother who had abandoned Theresa began a child custody case, which her wealthy new boyfriend financed. Theresa's dad was a simple blue-collar worker doing all he could to get by. Theresa's mother treated her new boyfriend's daughter far better than she treated her own daughter. Theresa never knew from day to day where she would spend the night.

I had spent an entire school year with a lost and wounded child and had never known it. I should have seen it. The failure I felt toward Theresa was unbearable. I could have done so much more for this wide-eyed child so lost in a cruel world. I earnestly prayed for forgiveness, feeling that I had not only failed Theresa, but God as well.

However, the grandfather's letter went on to say that the fact that I was Theresa's teacher had made the year beautiful for her. That because she had a safe haven in our classroom—a place where she knew she was loved and accepted—she was able to withstand the storms in the outside world. He told me I had changed her little life.

"When you are weak, then I am strong." That's what Jesus said. That's what this story proves. You may feel so inadequate, so incapable, like such a failure. But God can do all things—even use us to touch his little ones' lives when we're not aware of it.

Trust God. Stand firm in the knowledge that what he has begun in you—and your students—he will complete. You just never know.

Celebrate!

Celebrate God's touch
when you see it clearly in individual children

Give praise and glory to God for the small steps of faith you see your kids taking. Let the kids know you can see them growing. Don't hesitate to say things like:

"You helped me learn something about God today."

"I like to hear you pray—and God does too!"

"Wow! I never thought of that. Thanks for sharing with us."

"I could tell you were really worshiping God while we were singing."

"When you helped Peter with his project, you did just what God wants you to do!"

"You had a wonderful idea for our class project."

Celebrate God's touch
on your class as a whole

Build in ways for the kids to feel your affirmation and to affirm each other. Make sure each child leaves the room with a personal touch. You'll find examples of this in Godprints' *This Way Out* section at the close of the lessons. For instance, as kids leave the classroom, give each one a high-five and say, "I'll pray for Jackie today; today for Jackie I'll pray." Or have each child turn to the next one in line and give the promise of prayer.

> *And we, who with unveiled faces all reflect the Lord's glory, are being transformed into his likeness with ever-increasing glory, which comes from the Lord, who is the Spirit.*
>
> 2 Corinthians 3:18

Or, as kids leave your classroom, have each one look in a mirror and smile. Say, "Trust in God's plan, Chris. Trust in God's plan, Jake."

Look for opportunities to use individual names. You might have everyone shout, "Allison is precious to God." "Jeffrey is precious to God." Continue until you've used everyone's name.

Kick out of overdrive once each quarter to celebrate what kids have learned, how they've grown in faith, and how God has answered prayer. Party and praise God together! You'll love the ideas in Godprints' *Celebration FUNdays*. The last week of each quarter is set up to review and celebrate, and to invite other classes and parents to join you. Kids will look forward to demonstrating their newly gained knowledge. Parents will be happy to participate in games that review stories you've explored and the real-life applications you've discovered. And, of course, celebrate with food! Let kids make treats right in class to share with those who come.

Celebrate God's touch
on your class as a whole

Perhaps this is the year that you'll get the four year old who traumatized the nursery staff—and you'll teach him to love Sunday school and delight in God's Word. Perhaps this will be the year you have more kids than you feel you can handle—but with God's grace and wonderful helpers, you'll manage and succeed! Perhaps this will be the year you'll see something new in the Noah story you've taught 20 times, and you'll come away with an incredible sense of God's nearness and care.

God leaves his imprint on the kids you teach. And he leaves his imprint on you. God's touch is never static; it's always dynamic, always transforming. No one who truly encounters God is the same afterward.

Celebrate the GODPRINTS!
And thank YOU for loving God's kids.

Enjoy the mini-motivators on the pages that follow. Go to the copy store, pick out some wonderful paper and reproduce these pages for your own use, or to share with other teachers in your church. Use colored pencils and glitter glue to embellish the borders. Tuck the finished pieces in your Bible, frame them for your study, decoupage them, or just enjoy them here in the book. Return to this well of encouragement often!

My Calling, My Privilege, My Assurance

☀ ☀ ☀

Jesus said, "Let the little children come to me, and do not hinder them, for the kingdom of heaven belongs to such as these."

Matthew 19:14

Only be careful, and watch yourselves closely so that you do not forget the things your eyes have seen or let them slip from your heart as long as you live. Teach them to your children and to their children after them.

Deuteronomy 4:9

Keep his decrees and commands, which I am giving you today, so that it may go well with you and your children after you and that you may live long in the land the Lord your God gives you for all time.

Deuteronomy 4:40

We will not hide them from their children; we will tell the next generation the praiseworthy deeds of the Lord, his power, and the wonders he has done.

Psalm 78:4

Now go; I will help you speak and will teach you what to say.

Exodus 4:12

But the Counselor, the Holy Spirit, whom the Father will send in my name, will teach you all things and will remind you of everything I have said to you.

John 14:26

Whoever welcomes one of these little children in my name welcomes me; and whoever welcomes me does not welcome me but the one who sent me.

Mark 9:37

Celebrate God's Touch

Date_____ Today I saw God's touch in _____'s life.

Here's how: _____.

Date_____ Today I saw God's touch in _____'s life.

Here's how: _____.

Date_____ Today I saw God's touch in _____'s life.

Here's how: _____.

Date_____ Today I saw God's touch in _____'s life.

Here's how: _____.

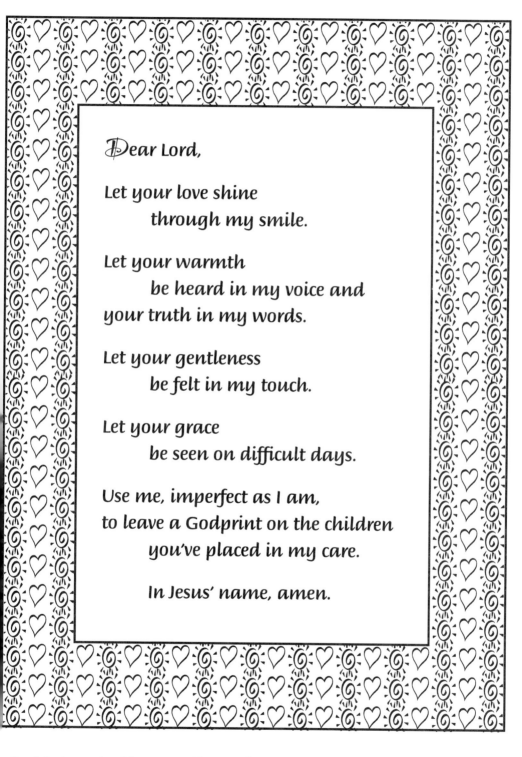

Dear Lord,

Let your love shine
    through my smile.

Let your warmth
    be heard in my voice and
your truth in my words.

Let your gentleness
    be felt in my touch.

Let your grace
    be seen on difficult days.

Use me, imperfect as I am,
to leave a Godprint on the children
    you've placed in my care.

In Jesus' name, amen.

Bibliography

Healy, Jane. *Your Child's Growing Mind.* New York: Doubleday, 1987, 1994.

Gardner, Howard. *Multiple Intelligences, The Theory in Practice.* New York: Basic Books, 1993.

Kotulak, Ronald. *Inside the Brain.* Kansas City: Andrews McMeel, 1996, 1997.

Seligman, Martin. *Learned Optimism.* New York: HarperPerennial, 1990, 1998.

Seligman, Martin. *The Optimistic Child.* New York: HarperPerennial, 1996.

Shapiro, Lawrence. *How to Raise a Child With a High EQ.* New York: Harper-Perennial, 1998.

Stonehouse, Catherine. *Joining Children On the Spiritual Journey.* Grand Rapids: Baker, 1998